DOG
DAYS
of History

The Incredible Story of **OUR BEST FRIENDS**

SARAH ALBEE

NATIONAL GEOGRAPHIC

WASHINGTON, D.C.

Contents

If you've picked up this book, then chances are you love dogs. If you have a dog, then you probably love her even when she barks her head off, or sneaks your sandwich off the counter, or throws up on your new sneakers.

What is it about dogs that humans love so much?

For starters, we love dogs because they love us back. They love us even when we've just scolded them for leaving muddy paw prints on the couch, or for chewing up our new baseball glove. We love dogs because they seem to sense when we're sad, or sick, or in need of a nuzzle.

So, what is it about humans that dogs love so much?

To answer that question, we must travel way, way back to prehistoric times, when humans first met canines. There's still a lot about the origins of dogs that scientists don't agree on. But we can make some safe assumptions about why the earliest dogs chose to "friend" us. Our bond most likely began as a practical partnership: Humans could provide dogs with food and warmth, thanks to our large brains, our ability to grasp stuff with our hands, and our skill at building a campfire. In turn, dogs could sound the alarm by barking when intruders approached. They could help us hunt with their speed, strength, and keen sense of smell. It was a win-win from the get-go.

But our relationship seems to have deepened quickly. It became something more complex, and it moved from a partnership to a friendship. Dogs are naturally affectionate, social animals. They love being around us.

From ancient times to the present, dogs have guarded us, worked with us, and marched off to war with us. They've saved our lives, kept us company, and helped us with daily tasks. And throughout the course of human history, dogs have loved us.

But there's an edgy quality to that love. That furry quadruped snuggling at your feet has a wild side. You might catch a glimpse of it when he snarls at another dog over a bone. Yet the next moment he seems to express almost human-like emotions, such as joy, sadness, or loneliness. Dogs occupy a middle space between the wilderness and civilization.

Over the centuries dogs have been both feared and prized. And because they have lived alongside us for thousands of years, their story is entwined with our story. So let's start at the beginning.

—*Sarah Albee*

 Our love for our dogs is unwavering. Most of the time.

The earliest known art showing humans and dog-like animals together was found in modern-day Algeria, in the Sahara before it became a desert. It dates back to somewhere between 6000 and 1500 B.C.

CHAPTER 1

BARKING
UP THE FAMILY TREE
From Wolf to Dog

Although modern dogs have been bred into all sorts of funny shapes and sizes, every dog you know is related to the wolf. Modern dogs share 99 percent of their DNA with the wolf. Dogs and wolves can still breed with one another, which means that from a scientific standpoint, they are the same species.

But when did dogs cross over from wild wolf to wolf-dog to dog-dog? And just when did they become domesticated? (See page 12.) Some scientists—the ones who study archaeology—think that dogs parted ways with wolves and began living with people about 15,000 years ago. Other scientists—the ones who study DNA—think dogs have been hanging around us much longer than that.

Dog Defined

So what is a dog, scientifically speaking? Dogs are members of the family Canidae, which includes about 35 species. They're carnivores (meat-eaters), although they also eat many plants and grains. They have five claws on their front paws and four on the back (although a few have a fifth rear claw), and they walk on their toes. Today, there are between 350 and 400 breeds of dog. A Labrador retriever might look entirely different from a spaniel, but they are both the same species.

The scientific name for any dog is *Canis lupus familiaris*. That officially makes it a subspecies of the modern wolf, which has the Latin name *Canis lupus*.

Paws
to
Consider

A species is a group of living things that can reproduce with one another. Their offspring can also produce offspring.

Close Cousins

Modern dogs have many close cousins around the world, including wild dogs, foxes, jackals, coyotes, and wolves. They all share a common ancestor, a prehistoric wolf, now extinct. Wolves and dogs probably diverged from the rest during the late Pleistocene epoch (about 35,000 years ago).

A unique type of wild dog is the Australian dingo. Scientists aren't sure how the dingo originally got to Australia. It may have originated in southern Asia about 6,000 years ago. About 4,000 years ago, some scientists believe semi-domesticated dingoes may have hitched a ride to Australia aboard Asian ships.

Some animals seem to be related to dogs but are not. Hyenas are actually closer to cats than they are to dogs. And, despite their name, prairie dogs are really rodents.

WOLF

COYOTE

JACKAL

DINGO

FOX

PRAIRIE DOG

HYENA

Even domesticated dogs sometimes display their wild origins.

What Does Domesticated Mean?

Do "tame" and "domesticated" mean the same thing? Not exactly. A lion tamer in the circus may "tame" a lion, and train her not to eat him, but her cubs will not be born tame.

Domestication happens over generations. An animal that is domesticated lives closely alongside humans, either as a pet or as a work animal. It is dependent on humans for food and shelter.

As the earliest dogs became domesticated over many generations, their appearance changed. Their coats grew softer, their ears floppier, their tails waggier. Their behavior changed, too. They grew less aggressive, and more sociable. They learned to read human gestures, and to obey human commands.

It's likely that certain dog-wolves had better survival odds than others. These were the animals that looked and behaved like cute, young animals. This adorableness trait is known as neoteny, which is a fancy word for keeping youthful features. The wolf pups who were more friendly and less fearful, and who had shorter snouts, bigger eyes, and softer fur, were more likely to be invited closer to the humans' campfire.

Where in the World?

Where and when did the first ancient wolves turn into dogs? Depends on which scientists you ask. Some say it happened in Europe. Others say Central Asia. Some say it happened 15,000 years ago. Others say 30,000. Many scientists now think dog domestication happened multiple times in multiple places around the world.

A Strait Shot? How Dogs Got to North America

That's one more thing scientists aren't sure about, because there are debates about how the first **people** got here. Most scientists believe that early dogs accompanied their humans from Asia into North America many thousands of years ago, when oceans were iced over and land bridges called straits stretched from one continent to another. But new studies have suggested that some Native Americans share DNA with Australians and Pacific Islanders. Could some early humans and dogs have arrived by ship? However dogs originally got to the Americas, they remained important to native people, serving as sled dogs, guards, and companions.

A 20th-century painting of Kiowa people and their dogs. These dogs probably resemble their North American ancestors.

Dogs Are Diverse

How could a tiny Chihuahua and a giant Great Dane be the same species? Dogs vary in size and shape more than any other species, mostly because of the way humans have bred them. There's only one other animal species that looks as different from one another as dogs do: humans.

Early on, humans figured out that if you deliberately breed a male and female dog that have certain desirable characteristics—such as speed, size, or intelligence—there is a much higher likelihood that their puppies will inherit those characteristics.

As a result, certain "types" of dogs have lived with humans since ancient times. These were working dogs, hunting dogs, war dogs, and pet (or lap) dogs. Because the design of a dog is so adaptable, it has become a constant partner to humans in every climate, from the frigid Arctic to the blazing desert.

Dog *breeds*, however, are a relatively modern development. You might think you recognize a greyhound on a Grecian urn, or a cocker spaniel in a Renaissance painting, but there's probably not a direct genetic link from the dogs you see on pottery and in paintings to those you know today. From one historical era to another, people bred dogs for similar purposes (working, fighting, guarding, and providing companionship). So while a direct link back to ancient times *may* exist, it's also possible that humans have created and re-created the same types of dogs.

Dogged Devotion

The famous collie, Lassie, played the ultimate devoted dog, in a long-running TV show.

As recently as the mid-20th century, dogs kept as pets were a luxury enjoyed mostly by the wealthy. Ordinary people didn't have time or space or money to take care of a pet dog. Just like their owners, dogs belonging to working families were expected to work for a living.

That has all changed in our day. Today more than 50 million American households own at least one pet dog.

As humans evolved over thousands of years, so did their dogs. This is the story of our constant companions, the faithful friends who have followed us through the centuries, all the way to the present day.

The hunting dogs in this 4,000-year-old image from ancient Egypt resemble the modern-day basenji breed.

CHAPTER 2

NO BONE UNTURNED

Dogs in the Ancient World

They appear on papyrus scrolls, Grecian urns, and Ming vases. Carved stone dogs from ancient Assyria snarl ferociously. Dogs were a big part of people's lives in ancient times. Some people even worshipped dogs. For many ancient cultures, dogs were more than a bridge between the wild and the civilized world. They also represented the bridge between the living and the dead. In one religion after another, people believed that dog-like deities (gods) helped the spirit of a dead person journey from this world to the next.

Dogs as Gods

In North America, the Aztec, Maya, Toltec, and Colima cultures all believed that dogs guided the dead person's soul to the underworld.

Carvings and images of Anubis—in the form of a jackal or dog—appear on monuments and tombs.

Ancient Egyptians believed that a dog-headed god named Anubis led souls to the other world. When a person died, Anubis would weigh the person's heart against the feather of truth. If heart and feather weighed the same, Anubis would escort the soul into the eternal afterlife. (If not, well, the heart got gobbled up by another god.) The Egyptians also named a bright star in the sky the Dog Star. (Later the Greeks and Romans would also call it Sirius.) The Dog Star was usually visible during the hottest part of the year, at the same time as the flooding of the Nile River.

The ancient Greeks believed the world of the dead was guarded by a three-headed dog named Cerberus.

In an ancient Indian legend, a king refused to enter heaven without his dog, even though it was against the rules. He was rewarded for his faithfulness, and the dog turned out to be a god in disguise.

Zooming Through Sumer

About 5000 B.C., one of the earliest civilizations, Sumer, arose in what is now part of Iraq and Kuwait. It was in the southern part of ancient Mesopotamia. The Sumerians are credited with inventing the wheel. They may have been the first society that used dogs to pull wheeled carts.

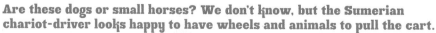

Are these dogs or small horses? We don't know, but the Sumerian chariot-driver looks happy to have wheels and animals to pull the cart.

Family Portraits

People in ancient times appreciated real dogs as much as god-dogs. Although they didn't understand genetics the way we do today, they knew that if a dog had long legs and good speed, it would make a good hunter, and that if it bred with another, equally long-legged, speedy dog, the offspring would also be excellent hunters. In every era, dog owners selected and bred dogs that were best suited to perform different tasks.

ANCIENT VARIETIES OF DOGS

THEN

NOW

The spitz-type dog had a curly tail, pointy ears, and, often, a rough, shaggy coat. It may have evolved in northern Arctic areas. It could withstand cold temperatures and had great strength and stamina.

The Molossus was a fierce, large, warrior dog that probably originated in southern Europe or Central Asia. These powerful dogs may be the ancestors of many modern breeds, including bulldogs, boxers, Saint Bernards, mastiffs, Rhodesian ridgebacks, and rottweilers.

THEN

NOW

THEN

NOW

The ancient Laconian hound was a "sight hound" or "gaze hound," prized for its sharp eyesight. These graceful animals were useful for hunting, and have been beloved by artists across the centuries.

 A faithful dog and its master. Even in ancient Egypt, treasured pet dogs had collars and leashes.

Mummy Dearest

From peasants all the way up to the pharaoh, the ancient Egyptians were big dog fans. Egyptians brought their dogs to work. They took them hunting. They pampered them as pets. Dogs pulled carts, herded animals, fought enemies, and carried loads. When a favorite dog died, members of the family sometimes shaved their eyebrows as a sign of mourning. Favorite dogs were often mummified alongside their owners. When discovered, some of the dogs still had mummified fleas and mummified ticks on them.

Egyptians were probably the first people to breed different kinds of dogs. We see examples of sleek, long-legged hunting types, and huge, muscular war dogs. The most commonly depicted dog in ancient Egyptian art is a hunting hound with pointy ears and a short curly tail. Dogs are frequently shown in domestic scenes, sitting by the chair of their master or mistress.

The days of intense summer heat that occurred when the Dog Star was visible were called "dog days" by many ancient cultures.

Thanks to ancient texts and collars found in tombs, we know some common names for dogs in ancient Egypt:

Good Herdsman

Reliable

Blackie

One Who Is Fashioned as an Arrow

Fourth

Sixth

Grabber

Cook-pot

She of the Town

Useless

Paws to Consider

Ancient Egyptian versions of "bow-wow" and "arf-arf" as translated by Egypt scholars include "abu-abu!" and "jw-jw!" (See page 102 for how dogs bark in other languages.)

Ancient Bodyguards

Throughout the ancient world, many royal heirs and nervous emperors felt in constant danger of being overthrown and killed—often by members of their own families. Faithful, obedient guard dogs were usually more trustworthy than human bodyguards who could be bribed.

Big dogs were prized for guard duty. They protected people, homes, and farm animals. Modern-day sheepdogs and mastiffs probably resemble their ancient cousins.

Guard dogs were used symbolically as well. Archaeologists have found dog-shaped talismans from many ancient civilizations that were believed to protect people's homes.

Even made of stone, this is a guard dog you would want to be wary of.

Assyrian War Dogs

Assyria was a fierce warrior society in Mesopotamia (now part of northern Iraq) that thrived for many centuries until its overthrow in about 610 B.C. Assyrians kept huge, mastiff-like hounds for hunting and for battle. This powerful, muscled dog breed was called the Molossus. Other warrior tribes also marched into battle with Molossian dogs, including the Hittites, Babylonians, and Greeks.

Assyrian artists were fond of depicting war scenes, including snarling dogs.

Cretan Canines

The Minoan civilization flourished from about 3000 B.C. to about 1100 B.C. (which was roughly the same time as the Egyptian Middle Kingdom) on the island of Crete, in the Mediterranean Sea. Unlike many of their neighbors, the Minoans were a peaceful civilization. There are very few scenes of war in the art that has survived, so they didn't have need for war dogs. In Minoan artwork, dogs are mostly pictured hunting. Some are shown guarding sacred tombs.

Classically Trained

The ancient Greeks both worshipped and feared dogs. In Athens, dogs were sometimes sacrificed to the gods. In the warrior society of Sparta, dogs were killed to ensure victory in battle. Life for common dogs tended to be as hard as it was for common people.

Wealthier Greeks did prize good hunting dogs, and many also owned guard dogs. (The less well-off used guard geese.)

Common street dogs were distrusted. As in many parts of the ancient world, homeless dogs roamed through the cities in packs, and threatened people walking in the streets. The disease called rabies was a very real threat and widely feared. (See page 55.) One bite from a "mad" dog could mean certain death, and everyone knew it. Dogs were banned from the Acropolis and other sacred places in Athens.

a beautiful image of a hound scratching its head, on a piece of Greek pottery from about 500 B.C.

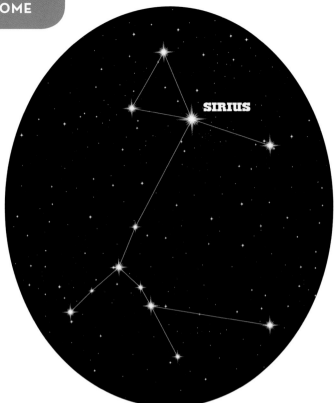

SIRIUS

Just as the Egyptians had done before them, the Greeks and Romans named constellations after dogs. We still call these constellations Canis Major and Canis Minor ("big dog" and "little dog"). The brightest star in Canis Major is also the brightest in the entire night sky—the star called Sirius. You can see it in the dawn sky in August—which is why its appearance marks the beginning of the "dog days" of summer.

Gladiator Days

The Greeks—and later the Romans—also used dogs for the popular sport known as animal baiting. (In the past, people had different ideas about what was fun than we do today.) Ferocious dogs were pitted against one another, or against wild animals like bears and lions, to fight to the death. Other giant breeds of dogs were trained to act as executioners. They were released inside the Roman Colosseum to slaughter prisoners, while the public watched. They were also used to battle with gladiators (armed fighters) for

sport. Crowds roared and cheered them on. The Roman Colosseum could seat 50,000 people—that's more than most modern baseball stadiums hold. Emperors encouraged this vicious entertainment and often paid for it. Free entertainment, they believed, would stop people from being bored, and also from criticizing the emperor.

a deadly contest in ancient Rome

No Place Like Rome

Roman war dogs could weigh 250 pounds (113 kg) and could knock an enemy off his horse. The dogs went into battle wearing spiked collars that were sharp as swords. Roman soldiers sometimes strapped pots filled with burning pitch (sticky resin) to the dogs' backs to scorch the bellies of horses and panic them in battle.

Wealthy Romans kept expensive and exotic kinds of dogs as status symbols. Images that were uncovered from the city of Pompeii, which was destroyed by a volcano in A.D. 79, picture guard dogs with the warning *Cave Canem* (Beware of Dog) in the entryways to private homes.

The poet Virgil, who lived from 70 to 19 B.C., urged his followers to keep a guard dog. With a dog on duty, he said, one never needs to "fear for your stalls a midnight thief, or onslaught of wolves, or Iberian brigands [thieves] at your back." A later writer suggested that buying a dog should be "among the first things which a farmer does, because it is the guardian of the farm, its produce, the household, and the cattle." He suggested that shepherds get an all-white dog to avoid mistaking it for a wolf in the half-light of dawn or dusk, and that farmers get an all-black guard dog for the farm to terrify thieves in the daytime and be less visible to trespassers at night.

Small dogs served as companion dogs for people of leisure. Long-bodied, feisty dogs were speedy enough to run down small animals in a hunt. Called *vestigators*, they resembled modern-day terriers.

A guard dog mosaic on the floor of a grand house in Pompeii, from the first century A.D. The artist created it by arranging small pieces of colored tile into a picture.

Celtic Canines

The Celts (pronounced KELTS) were a group of warrior tribes that lived at the same time as the ancient Romans in what is now Great Britain. The Celts also used dogs in battle. Their massive dogs wore spiked collars and quilted cloaks to protect them from arrows. The Celts were also enthusiastic hunters, and used "swifthounds" (which resemble today's mastiff breeds) to track down wild boar and other game. After the Romans invaded Celtic Britain, they learned a lot from the Celts about dog training and hunting.

The Celts also used terriers, bred to pursue prey underground. Eventually Roman guard dogs and Celtic hunting dogs bred and formed some gentler breeds.

Look carefully at this Celtic brooch. Can you see the dogs in the pattern?

Paws to Consider

The Canary Islands were named by the ancient Romans for the wild dogs that roamed there. (*Canis* is Latin for dog.) Canaries—the songbirds—were named after the islands later, not the other way around.

27

Hairless Dogs

The Maya civilization in Mesoamerica flourished, on and off, for a few thousand years. The heyday for the civilization peaked around A.D. 250, when large, independent kingdoms spread across Mexico, Guatemala, Honduras, and Belize. Many Maya kept dogs for hunting and herding.

In the Colima culture of western Mexico, peculiar-looking, hairless, potbellied dogs lived with their humans and were both worshipped and sacrificed to please the gods. The pudgy dogs are often depicted in sculpture in playful poses.

The Xoloitzcuintli (pronounced show-low-eet-squint-lee, or Xolo for short) is a similar type of hairless dog. Its name comes from the Aztec god Xolotl, and the Aztec word for dog, *itzcuintli*. The Aztec, who lived in what is now Mexico from the 13th to the 16th centuries, believed the dogs were sacred. They believed that the god Xolotl created the hairless dog to protect and guide humans.

🐾 **the ancient Colima dog (chubby and cherished)**

🐾 **the modern Xoloitzcuintli (say THAT five times fast!)**

Lion Dogs

The lion is an important symbol of the Buddhist faith. But in ancient China, lions were hard to come by. So, royal dog breeders hit upon a solution: Dogs were bred to *look* like lions. The more lion-like a dog could look, the more revered was the dog. And because small dogs were considered lucky, the Pekinese (or Pekingese, named after China's capital of Peking—now Beijing) made ideal mini-lions. (See page 71 for what became of the Pekinese breed.)

Yappy Days

The original lapdogs—literally, dogs that were small enough to sit on your lap—were bred in China, Tibet, and Japan. They were also known as sleeve dogs, because many were small enough to fit into the hanging sleeves of robes and kimonos. They made great hand-warmers.

You can sense real affection between the woman and her small, perky dog, which the artist placed at the center of the picture.

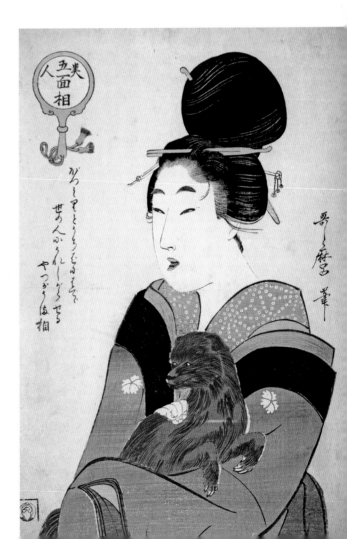

Christine de Pisan was a renowned French writer, at a time when few women could earn a living as writers. In this scene, painted about 1410, her devoted little dog sits adoringly at her feet.

CHAPTER 3

MASTIFFS, MUTTS, AND MAD DOGS

Dogs in the Middle Ages

The Middle Ages, also known as medieval times, were a period in Western history that happened after the fall of the Roman Empire and before the Renaissance (roughly A.D. 500 to 1400). This period probably makes you think of moats, castles, and pointy princess hats. In reality, nobly-born knights, lords, and ladies made up a tiny percentage of the population. Most people were peasants who spent their lives living in squalor, toiling in the fields, and trying not to die from disease, starvation, or childbirth. Although dogs owned by the nobility enjoyed a relatively comfortable existence, life for most medieval-era dogs wasn't any easier than it was for the rest of the population.

A-Hunting We Will Go (But You Won't)

In medieval Europe, about 97 percent of the people were peasants, ruled over by a duke or lord, who in turn reported to the king. The king had absolute power. He could grant land and titles to favored members of the nobility. Commoners rarely owned the land they farmed.

One of the most popular pastimes for the wealthy was hunting. Hunting groups might include over a hundred hounds. Prized hunting dogs were cared for in the kennels by "dog-boys," who usually lived in the kennel, sleeping alongside the dogs.

Many of the well-to-do also kept dogs as pets and companions. For long hours of sermons in unheated churches, a small dog could be an excellent foot-warmer or lap-warmer. It was also handy to sleep with in a cold, drafty bedroom.

But owning hunting dogs and companion dogs were rare luxuries. In most parts of Europe, only the king and his nobles were allowed to hunt game, and they hunted with hounds, mastiffs, and spaniels. Commoners kept dogs for protection and to herd animals, but it was usually against the law for commoners to use dogs for hunting.

In 12th-century England, peasants were allowed to own curs (see Paws to Consider, below) and terriers, but their dogs had to be small enough to pass through a metal hoop. If a peasant owned a big dog to defend his home, the law demanded that it had to be hobbled to prevent it from hunting. That meant that three of its toes were cut off. If your dog was discovered unhobbled, you could be suspected of being a poacher (someone who hunts animals for food illegally). As you might imagine, this cruel law did not go over very well with medieval dog owners.

Paws to Consider

The word "cur" comes from a medieval law that required "regular" dogs to have their tails cropped ("courtailed") so that they wouldn't be confused with aristocratic hunting dogs. The word was shortened to "curtal" and finally to "cur." Nowadays it's a word that describes an unappealing mixed-breed dog, or a human scoundrel.

Later, in France, King Francis I ordered that all dogs owned by peasants and farmers have a heavy block of wood attached to their collars, to prevent them from running after game animals. To make matters worse, many hunt-loving rulers expanded their hunting grounds and swallowed up lands occupied by farms, churches, and communities, forcing residents to move out. Medieval game wardens called verderers were given the task of enforcing these hated hunting laws. Often they took bribes in exchange for not arresting poachers, and they were universally despised by common people.

Nothing but a Hound Dog

William the Conqueror came from Normandy, France. He and his troops invaded England in 1066 and fought a battle with the English known as the Battle of Hastings. The Norman invaders brought the bloodhound with them to England. Many of the prized hounds had been raised by monks at a French abbey called Saint Hubert. These dogs are pictured in the famous Bayeux Tapestry (below), which depicts the battle. The Normans won, and French was spoken in the court of England for the next 300 years. Owning a Saint Hubert hound became a big status symbol with the nobility in medieval England.

hunting hounds in a detail of the Bayeux Tapestry

In this 12th-century medical text, a crowsfoot plant is recommended for treating a dog bite.

Dogs and the Black Death

In the 14th century, a deadly and highly contagious disease known as the Black Death wiped out as much as a third of the population of Europe. Similar grim death tolls occurred in the Middle East and northern Africa. Although no one knew it at the time, this disease, now called bubonic plague, was spread by the bite of a diseased flea. Dogs seemed to have some resistance to the plague, unlike other animals and people, so they were believed to play a part in its spread. During bad outbreaks, city officials ordered dogs to be rounded up and destroyed. Many fairy tales and legends that featured werewolves and other fearful dog-like creatures originated during the Middle Ages.

WORDS OF ADVICE FROM MEDIEVAL TIMES

➡ WATCH OUT FOR WOLVES!

In case you cross paths with a wolf, medieval scholars at the British Library have translated this questionable advice from a 13th-century writer:

If the wolf sees you before you see the wolf, you will probably lose your ability to speak or cry for help.
There is only one cure for this condition. You must quickly take off all your clothes, throw them on the ground and trample them. Then you must pick up two stones and bang them together to make a loud noise—only then will your power of speech be restored!

What Big Teeth They Had: Fear of Wolves

If dogs toed the line between the wilderness and the civilized world for people of the Middle Ages, then wolves walked on the wild side. Wolf-hunting was usually a ruler's one exception to the hunting ban. Anyone, even a peasant, was allowed to hunt wolves. We know now that dogs and wolves are the same species, but in the typical medieval person's mind, a wolf prowling the dangerous wilderness might actually be a supernatural creature. Wolves roamed the forests that covered much of northern Europe, and they were greatly feared. The wolf character is the bad guy in many fables, legends, and fairy tales—from ancient times (Aesop's *Boy Who Cried Wolf*), to medieval times (*Little Red Riding Hood*), to the 19th century (*Three Little Pigs*).

Wolfhounds—dogs that hunted wolves—were often presented to rulers as gifts. Edward I (1272–1307), king of England, ordered the wholesale extermination of wolves in his realm. By about 1500, wolves had almost completely disappeared from Europe and Britain.

Sadly, the irrational fear of wolves has carried through to today, and these intelligent, social animals are endangered species in many parts of the world.

The tale of Little Red Riding Hood and her encounter with the Big Bad Wolf has been terrifying young children for centuries.

35

Setting the Scene

Around A.D. 800, while medieval Europeans were suffering from war, poverty, and disease, the Chinese empire grew in size, strength, and wealth. Chinese inventions like paper, movable type, and gunpowder advanced communication and warfare, and science, art, philosophy, and architecture flourished. In China, chow chow dogs guarded temples from evil spirits. Emperors and nobles kept dogs as pets. And war dogs fought alongside soldiers.

In A.D. 1234, nomadic invaders from a region northwest of China called Mongolia invaded and overthrew the ruling dynasty in China. They conquered more and more territories. From the late 12th to the late 14th centuries, the Mongols ruled over the largest empire in history.

Genghis Khan—in the Middle Ages the title "Khan" meant "supreme ruler."

Dogs of War

Early Mongols were nomadic tribes who lived on horseback and moved between summer and winter pasture lands. Then Genghis Khan (1167-1227) rose up to rule—mostly by killing anyone who stood in his way—and unified the Mongols.

Genghis Khan claimed that he was descended from the union of a gray wolf and a white doe. His armies were so feared that many terrified rulers in their path surrendered without a fight.

The Mongol warriors brought dogs with them as they thundered through Asia on horseback. Stories and legends grew about how Genghis Khan's "armies" of Tibetan mastiffs, originally from the foothills of the Himalaya, helped him conquer most of Central Asia, from Beijing to the Caspian Sea and eastern Europe. He even called his four greatest (human) generals the Dogs of War.

Thousands of Hounds, and Other Imperial Pooches

In 1279, Genghis Khan's grandson, Kublai Khan (1215-1294), defeated what remained of China and expanded the Mongol empire even farther, across much of Southeast Asia. His lavish court was visited by a number of Europeans, the most famous of whom was a Venetian trader named Marco Polo. Polo claimed to have arrived in 1275, and later

Kublai Khan and a royal hound, in a hunting scene

wrote about his trip. He seemed especially fascinated with the dogs he saw during his travels. Some historians believe he never made it as far as China, and just relied on accounts of travelers who had. But many of his dog stories proved to be reasonably factual.

Polo claimed that Kublai Khan had 10,000 hunting hounds. Although some historians think that number might be slightly exaggerated, there were certainly enough dogs to help hunters supply the royal kitchens with a thousand birds and beasts a day to feed the people of the court.

In his accounts, Polo also described large guard dogs used by people in Tibet that were "as big as donkeys." He noted that in one province of Kublai Khan's kingdom, "the country swarms with lions." He wrote about a fierce breed of dog that was used to protect travelers from lion attacks: "So every man who goes a journey takes with him a couple of those dogs, and when a lion appears they have at him with the greatest boldness, and the lion turns on them, but can't touch them for they are very deft at eschewing his blows."

After Kublai Khan's death, the power of the Mongolian empire gradually declined.

Paws to Consider

The thick-coated, curly-tailed snow dog known as the Akita is associated with northern Japan. They may have arrived with hunters 2,000 years ago. Known for their courage, loyalty, and fierce fighting spirit, the dogs served as a source of inspiration to samurai—the warrior class. During feudal times, only the emperor and members of the aristocracy were permitted to own an Akita. Special leashes signaled the Akita owner's status. (See Hachiko, page 82.)

The Renaissance artist named Titian (TISH-un) included many dogs in his paintings. His portrait of a powerful Italian duke and his dog shows the duke's tender side.

CHAPTER 4

TOUGH TIMES, RUFF TIMES

Dogs of the Renaissance

The Renaissance was a period of European history that began about 1400 and lasted until about 1630. Literally meaning "rebirth," the Renaissance was a time of renewed interest in science, art, music, and invention. World exploration expanded, and many European rulers jostled for the right to "discover" new lands and establish new colonies, without worrying too much about the fact that people were already living in these places. It was also a time of extreme contrasts, not only for humans, but also for their dogs.

 A young future king of England, Charles II, with his dogs and siblings. The enormous mastiff dog dominates the painting.

The Lucky Few

For dogs belonging to people in the upper ranks of society, life was good. Dogs continued to be bred for members of the nobility to go hunting and hawking (or, for a change of pace, falconing), and were kept as pampered pets and companions. Renaissance artists put these dogs into paintings to symbolize loyalty, obedience, and faithfulness. (People at the top of the social ladder were probably pretty keen on encouraging loyalty, obedience, and faithfulness in their underlings.) In contrast, wolves in art often represented greed and savagery.

The dogs of the wealthy might be pressed into service as bed-warmers, foot-warmers, lap-warmers, and even poison-tasters. They could also be handy stand-ins as napkins because people ate with their fingers—forks weren't in general use until well into the 1600s.

Working Like a Dog, Renaissance Style

The inequality between the well-to-do and everyone else was reflected in dogs as well. Dogs that belonged to people who worked for a living led very different lives from their pampered cousins. For most common dogs, work was hard and food was meager, just as it was for their masters. Dogs toiled inside large wheels (see below), which turned meat spits, churned butter, and ground grain. They pulled carts, chased and killed rats, and herded livestock. Performing dogs did tricks. Fighting dogs "baited" bulls or other dogs, just as they'd done in ancient Greek and Roman times, and people placed bets on who would win these vicious fights.

Because there were no police and plenty of violent crimes, guard dogs were especially popular, for both rich and poor.

Turnspit Dogs

During the Renaissance, when meat was roasted over an open kitchen fire, someone needed to turn it on a spit for even cooking. Sometimes young boys were used for this hot, dangerous job, but in many grand houses and estates, cooks used dogs. Turnspit dogs were put into a treadmill like a hamster in a wheel, which was attached to a rotating device. When the dog turned the treadmill, the treadmill turned the spit. Long-bodied, "crooked-legged" breeds were used, and sometimes they might work in teams, alternating shifts on different days. And these dogs didn't even get Sundays off. People often brought them to church to act as foot-warmers.

According to a 16th-century writer, "Turnspetes" could also be used for street circus performances, having been "taught to dance to the drums and to the lyre."

Can you spot the dog turning the wheel in the upper part of this picture?

Run, Spot, Run!

"There is also this day among us a newe kind of dogge brought out of Fraunce ... speckled all over with white and black," said a book on dogs written at the time of Queen Elizabeth I. Dalmatians probably originated in the Dalmatia province of the former Yugoslavia. They got along well with horses. In Britain, these spotted dogs became known as "English coach dogs." Because of their strength and stamina, and their ability to get along with horses, Dalmatians ran alongside horse-drawn carriages. Later, they became associated with firefighting because their loud bark cleared bystanders out of the way. They stood watch at fires and guarded the equipment from thieves.

Dalmatians and other strong, fast dogs became something of a status symbol for the wealthy. They stood guard over people's belongings when travelers rested for the night.

Dalmatian puppies are born white. The spots develop a few weeks later.

Reigning Cats and Dogs

Doomed Dog

Henry VIII's second wife, Anne Boleyn, had a little dog named Purkoy—from the French *pourquoi*, which means "why?" (Evidently the dog was very curious.) Purkoy died mysteriously of a fall from a high window only a few months after being given to the queen. Anne was not popular in the palace, and some speculate the death may not have been an accident.

 Anne Boleyn (right) and Mary Queen of Scots (below)

Friend to the End

Henry VIII's daughter, Elizabeth I, ascended the throne in 1558. Mary Queen of Scots, a cousin of the queen, believed she had a stronger claim to the throne. Elizabeth ordered Mary to be arrested and put in prison. After many years of conflicted feelings, Elizabeth finally signed the warrant for Mary's death.

As Mary approached the execution block, a witness reported that the executioner "espied her little dog which was crept under her clothes, which could not be gotten forth but by force." After Mary was beheaded, the dog was given to one of Mary's friends, a French princess.

Sixteenth-century Europeans described some native North American dogs as "fox-like," as in this 1840 etching.

Old World Dogs Meet New World Dogs

The Renaissance was a time when Europeans embarked on far-flung expeditions around the world. Sailors brought dogs along to keep them company on long voyages and guard ships while at anchor.

Spain and Portugal were major world powers at the end of the 15th and early 16th centuries. Intent on acquiring gold to fund their many wars, Spanish and Portuguese monarchs sent conquistadors (explorers) to the New World.

Dogs did exist in the New World before the arrival of Europeans, but they were small. The natives had never seen huge dogs like the wolfhounds and mastiffs brought over by the conquistadors.

Trained for Terror

Throughout history, humans have at times taken advantage of dogs' willingness to do anything for their masters by training them for evil purposes. Perhaps one of the worst instances of such abuses of dogs' loyalty happened in the European conquest of the New World.

The cruel conquistadors often used huge, vicious dogs that had been trained to kill as weapons against the native people, and to frighten them into bringing them gold.

Christopher Columbus brought 20 dogs with him on his second voyage to the New World, in 1493. He used dogs to terrify the native people of what was modern-day Jamaica, and, later, Hispaniola (modern-day Dominican Republic). Hernán Cortés used dogs to frighten the Aztec people. Hernando de Soto brought dogs to Florida and Mississippi. Francisco Pizarro used them to conquer the Inca. Ponce de León trained dogs to attack rebellious natives in Puerto Rico. Balboa, Velásquez, and Coronado would all use the same tactics. It's one of the most brutal chapters in the history of humans and dogs.

 A rather inaccurate depiction of Spanish conquistadors and their dainty-looking dogs. Their real dogs were large, fierce, and trained to attack.

A portrait of an English baronet and his noble dog. The artist, Sir Joshua Reynolds, was a famous painter of the Enlightenment who often included dogs in his portraits.

CHAPTER 5

ENLIGHTENMENT DOGS

The 17th and 18th Centuries

The Age of Enlightenment was notable for scientific discovery, new inventions, and revolutions. For humans, that is. Dogs were unaware of all that. But they were there to comfort famous Enlightenment thinkers like Isaac Newton as he toiled in his laboratory, as well as doomed monarchs like King Charles I as he faced his execution. They posed for portrait painters. They were coiffed and curled into unwitting symbols of wealth and aristocracy. And, as ever, dogs continued to help working people by hauling, guarding, hunting, and protecting. But the winds of democratic change were beginning to blow.

An example of a dog hitched to a travois in an 1890 photograph of a Tsuu T'ina chief and his wife

Native Dogs

Before the arrival of European settlers, dogs were Native Americans' only domesticated animals.

Many native societies revered dogs. Certain groups of Native Americans sometimes sacrificed them for the protection they believed the dogs would give them.

Horses were unknown in North America until they were imported by the Spanish in the early 1500s. To carry their belongings, Native Americans used dogs to pull sleds. Two wooden poles were attached to the back of the dog, who pulled the load at the other end along the ground.

The sleds became known by the French-Canadian word "travois" (pronounced trav-WAH or trah-VOY). The Ojibwa word is *niswaakodaabaan* (niss-wah-ko-dah-bahn), and the Lakota Sioux word is *hupak'in* (hoo-POCK-een).

Fetching Names

Some common names for Algonquian dogs:

Baby

Little Pin

Sauce

Ask Him

Try Him

Where's That?

Hoot Owl

Clown

Bear

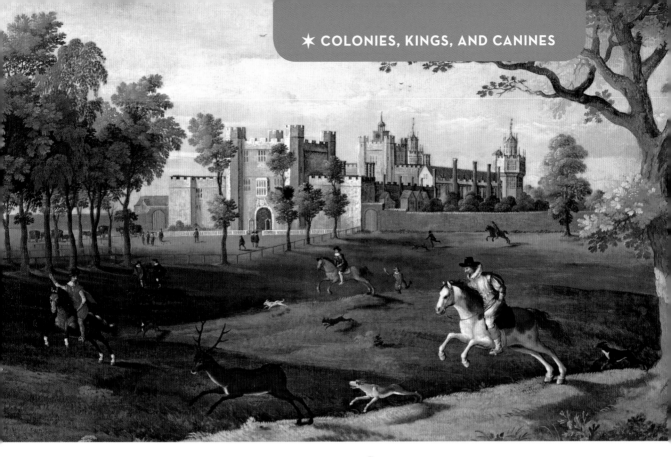

King James I, an unpopular monarch, having fun hunting

Clueless Kings

The first permanent English settlement in the American colonies, Jamestown, was named after the English king James I (1566–1625). The king was crazy about hunting. And like so many of his royal predecessors, he seemed to put his own hunting fun ahead of the needs of his subjects. He demanded that farmers take down fences, and he often seized their dogs and added them to his own hunting dog stable.

James was succeeded by his son, Charles I (1600–1649), and Charles was even less popular than his father had been. Charles continued the cruel practice of ordering large dogs to be hobbled so they wouldn't be able to chase after his game. He angered his Protestant subjects by marrying a French princess, and then dissolved Parliament when its members opposed him. His subjects revolted in 1642, and he was beheaded in 1649. His little spaniel, Rogue, was permitted to follow him across the park on his walk to his execution.

Later in the century, the monarchy was restored. Charles I's son, Charles II (1630–1685), assumed the throne. Charles II was so fond of dogs he allowed them the run of his palace, to the private annoyance of many. One diarist was appalled that the king let dogs give birth to puppies right in the royal bedchamber. The large number of dogs in the palace "render'd it very offensive and indeed made the whole Court nasty and stinking." The Cavalier King Charles spaniel is named after him.

Dogs on Deck

In 1607, a small group of English settlers arrived in what would become Jamestown, Virginia, to establish the first permanent English colony in the New World. But four years *before* that, an Englishman named Martin Pring came to the New World and explored the coastlines of what would eventually be Maine, New Hampshire, and Massachusetts. He would later publish his maps and writings, which had a lot to do with sparking people's interest in exploring the new land. But he might not have made it back to England without the presence of his two huge dogs, Foole and Gallant.

Pring's two ships, the *Discoverer* and the *Speedwell,* arrived off the coast of Cape Cod. They were there to collect sassafras, a leaf that the Europeans prized for its medicinal qualities. "We brought from Bristoll two excellent Mastives, of whome the Indians were more afraid, then of twentie of our men." The Wampanoag (pronounced wom-puh-NO-ahg) had not seen the likes of such huge dogs. At one point a group of warriors seemed to be on the verge of attacking Pring and his men, but spotted the "great and fearfull Mastives," and "turned all to a jest and sport," and retreated, allowing Pring and his men to sail back to England.

Seventeen years later, the *Mayflower* arrived. On it were at least two dogs, a mastiff and a spaniel.

Pilgrim Pooches

You may have learned that the English settlers were taught how to fertilize corn seedlings by burying them with a small fish. A Wampanoag man whom the Europeans called Squanto did teach the Pilgrims this practice, but it now seems unlikely that the native people routinely farmed this way. Squanto may have learned this practice while living in Europe. But it seemed to work for the Pilgrims. To keep dogs from digging up the fish, one of the dog's front paws was tied to a string around its neck for forty days after planting.

Puritan Pooches

As more English settlers arrived in the New World, they brought dogs with them. Dogs hunted, herded, and turned spits, bellows, and churns. At Puritan meeting houses (the Puritans' word for church), dogs kept people's feet warm during day-long Sunday services.

But not everyone looked kindly on those furry foot-warmers. Just as they'd done back in England, many parishes employed "dog whippers." Their job was to control unruly dogs brought to church by worshippers, and to shoo away strays that wandered in. Puritan dog whippers also woke people who'd dozed off. (They were called "sluggard wakers.") They even whacked at squirming children. Sermons lasted for hours in unheated rooms on uncomfortable benches, so the dog whippers/sluggard wakers had their work cut out for them. By 1635, the Massachusetts colony made it a crime to bring a dog into a meeting house.

A Puritan meeting house in colonial New England. No dogs allowed.

Getting Philosophical

Back across the Atlantic, Enlightenment philosophers, poets, and scientists (called "natural philosophers") embraced the growing enthusiasm for dogs as creatures worthy of our love. The French writer A. Toussenel wrote: "The more one gets to know of man, the more one values dogs." The English poet and essayist Alexander Pope said that "histories are more full of examples of fidelity of dogs than of friends." Even fleas began to command some respect.

 Alexander Pope had a faithful dog named Bounce.

Scratch Scratch

Where there have been dogs, there have been fleas. And so the flea has played a significant role in human history. Besides causing annoying, itchy bites, the flea has created much bigger problems for us. One species of flea transmits a form of plague (see page 34), and that disease has led to the deaths of millions of people over the centuries.

Is there an upside to the flea? The first to look at a flea under a microscope was Galileo Galilei, in 1624. Forty years later, the scientist Robert Hooke drew a picture of a magnified flea, in beautiful detail. The flea has inspired love poems, songs, and paintings.

The English poet John Donne wrote a love poem entitled "The Flea," published in 1633, in which a flea bites both himself and his beloved. It begins:

Mark but this flea, and mark in this,
How little that which thou deniest me is;
It sucked me first, and now sucks thee,
And in this flea our two bloods mingled be ...

In the Doghouse

The famous English scientist Isaac Newton was not exactly a people person. His closest relationship may have been with his dog, a white Pomeranian named Diamond. One of the most recounted stories of Newton (second only to his purportedly getting bonked on the head by an apple and coming up with his theory of gravity), is how sometime in the late 1680s, his little dog knocked over a candle and set Newton's manuscript on fire. It destroyed years of Newton's life work. It took him at least a year to rewrite the manuscript, but he forgave Diamond. (Some scholars think this story might be made-up.)

A dramatic depiction of Diamond's destruction (above). A portrait of Sir Isaac Newton in a calmer moment (below).

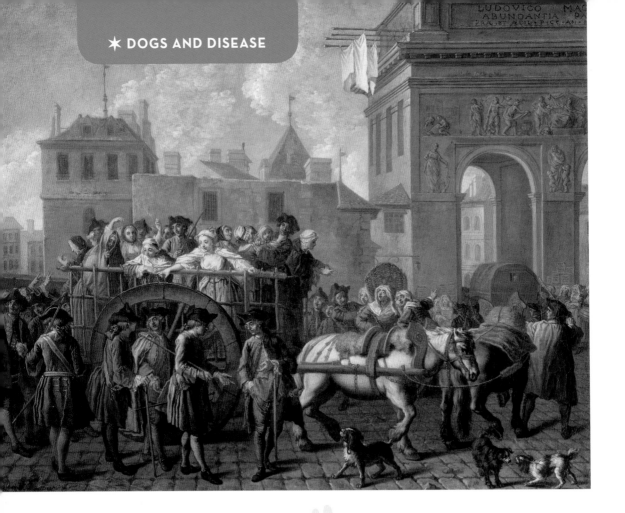

Dogs, horses, and other animals added to the bustle of 18th-century Paris streets. Can you spot all the walking sticks?

Pack Attacks

As 18th-century cities grew larger, the populations of animals increased along with their human inhabitants. Animals were everywhere. With no refrigeration, live animals had to be close at hand to supply butchers with meat. Herds of cattle were driven through city streets. Horses clopped, pigs rooted through garbage, herds of livestock were driven to markets, and stray dogs roamed everywhere.

So, city streets were not serene places to go walking. There were no sidewalks. Most streets were unpaved. Slaughterhouses, tanneries, and bone-boilers contributed dreadful smells to the air. Thousands of animals per year dropped dead, usually from natural causes, but dead cows, horses, pigs, cats, and dogs were left to rot in poorer neighborhoods. As the fashion for gentlemen wearing swords went out of style, swords were replaced with walking sticks. No doubt the walking sticks came in handy to whack away packs of dogs.

Butchers in Boston got sick of stray dogs stealing meat. In 1728, the city banned dogs that were taller than 10 inches. The real fear about unruly dogs, though, was rabies.

Rabies Revisited

We know now that rabies is a viral disease, which can be transmitted to a person who gets bitten by an infected dog or a wild animal like a fox or a bat. But it wasn't until the 19th century that Louis Pasteur figured out how to prevent it (see page 72). People of the 18th century had no cure for the disease, and it was deeply feared. Once the symptoms of rabies appeared, the disease was nearly always fatal.

Of course there were plenty of theories about how rabies originated. Some believed dogs could get it "because they feed upon carrion and corrupt, putride and stinking things, and lap water of the like condition." Others thought it was caused by excessive thirstiness. Others were sure it was tied to the position of the stars and planets in the night sky.

The disease was terrifying, and painful. Symptoms could last for up to three weeks. They began with headache and fever, but as the disease progressed, the virus attacked the central nervous system and caused involuntary spasms, mania ("madness"), and fear of water. Fear of water is also known as hydrophobia.

People knew how to recognize a mad dog. It "hath sparkling and fierie eies, with a fixed looke, cruell and a squint, hee carries his head heavily, hanging downe towards the ground, and somewhat on one side, hee gapes, and thrusts forth his tongue, which is livide and blackish; and being short breathed, casts forth much filth at his nose, and much foaming matter at his mouth."

Dubious remedies for the bite of a mad dog were also plentiful. One popular belief was that getting dunked in water might cure you. One writer suggested that the patient's head should be held under water three or four times "for as long as ye party can bear it."

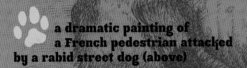

a dramatic painting of a French pedestrian attacked by a rabid street dog (above)

a young girl and
her small dog, both
extremely well-groomed

Pampered Pets

In the years leading up to the French Revolution, members of the French nobility dressed in ever more outrageous fashions at the court of Versailles (pronounced vayr-SYE). Fashionable ladies employed canine stylists to pamper their dogs. These stylists, called "demoiselles," bathed, clipped, and styled dogs' fur into coiffures nearly as elaborate as those of their mistresses. But, as ever, the nobility frowned upon dogs owned by ordinary people. In 1770 the king imposed a heavy tax on commoners' dogs, which added to the people's growing resentment. After the revolution and the overthrow of the French monarchy, many members of the nobility, including the king and queen, were executed by guillotine. Many fancy dogs were executed along with their owners.

General George
Washington, dog lover

General Considerations

Over in America, overtaxed colonists had declared their desire for independence from Great Britain. The commander of the Continental Army was George Washington.

On October 6, 1777, General Washington's army lost a battle at Germantown, Pennsylvania, to British forces. After the battle, the American soldiers found a confused little dog on the battlefield. The inscription on the collar said that it belonged to the British commander, General William Howe. Washington arranged for a messenger to return the dog, with this note:

General Washington's compliments to General Howe. He does himself the pleasure to return him a dog, which accidentally fell into his hands, and by the inscription on the Collar appears to belong to General Howe.

Evidently General Howe was overjoyed to have his dog returned.

POOCHES IN PORTRAITS

During the 18th century, fancy dogs became more and more of a status symbol. Just as in the past, they were used as props for portraits. Many gentlemen had their portraits painted with their hand upon the head of a faithful dog, to make themselves appear more masterful and powerful. Ladies had their portraits painted with their lapdogs, which were also important fashion accessories. As one London magazine writer grumbled, "servants to Ladies of Quality are washing and combing such lap-dogs as are to go to church with their mistresses that morning." Children of the well-to-do were also painted with dogs.

But with the 18th century came a new trend: dog portraits, where dogs were not just part of the picture—they were the *only* subject. The rising status of dogs was reflected in the new dog accessories that became available, such as fancy beds and collars.

A new trend for portrait painters—dogs took center stage.

Sweet Lips and
Madame Moose

George Washington (President 1789–1797)

George Washington was a dog lover. At his home in Virginia, called Mount Vernon, he kept a variety of dogs, including hunting hounds, spaniels, terriers, greyhounds, Dalmatians, and at least one Newfoundland. Many had silly names, including Sweet Lips, Mopsey, and Madame Moose.

Pete

Theodore Roosevelt (President 1901–1909)

Theodore Roosevelt had many pet dogs during his time as president. One of his dogs, a bull terrier named Pete, menaced the White House for several years. Pete's job was to patrol the grounds of the White House and chase away intruders. Pete often took the job too far. In 1905, Pete chased the French ambassador up a tree, possibly even tearing the backside of the man's pants. He was banished to a nearby farm for an extended doggie time-out. There are no photos of Pete, but he probably looked like the bull terrier at the right.

Laddie Boy

Warren G. Harding (President 1921–1923)

During his presidency, Warren G. Harding was plagued with problems. Many in his inner circle were accused of corruption. But at least one member of his administration enjoyed great popularity with the American people: his dog, Laddie Boy. The Airedale terrier delivered the newspaper to the president every morning, and frequently sat in on meetings.

After Harding died in office from an illness, an artist designed a Laddie Boy sculpture made from 19,000 pennies, in honor of the president and his loyal dog. The pennies were donated by newspaper delivery boys around the country. It's still part of the collection of the Smithsonian Museum today.

Fala

Franklin D. Roosevelt (President 1933–1945)

Franklin D. Roosevelt's Scottish terrier, Fala, was a fun-loving little dog who often entertained White House visitors with adorable tricks. Fala made headlines during FDR's 1944 reelection campaign, when Republicans falsely claimed that Fala had been left behind on an island and that Roosevelt had spent millions of taxpayers' dollars sending a naval destroyer ship to retrieve him. Roosevelt hotly denied the story in a now-famous speech, where he complained: "These Republican leaders have not been content with attacks on me, or my wife, or on my sons. No, not content with that, they now include my little dog, Fala."

Pushinka

John F. Kennedy (President 1961–1963)

Eight months after the Russians successfully sent two dogs into space (see page 91), one of the two astronaut-dogs, Strelka, gave birth to a litter of puppies. The leader of the Soviet Union, Nikita Khrushchev, gave one of Strelka's puppies to Caroline Kennedy, the young daughter of President John F. Kennedy. The white, mixed-breed puppy's name was Pushinka, which is Russian for "fluffy."

Checkers

Richard M. Nixon (President 1969–1974)

In 1952, when Richard Nixon was running for vice president alongside Dwight Eisenhower for president, he was accused of accepting gifts improperly. He gave a speech on television—a relatively new-fangled appliance in most homes—and denied the accusations. He did admit that his family had kept one gift: a dog. "And our little girl, Tricia, the six-year-old, named it Checkers." The awkward, stiff-seeming Nixon showed his human side, and the speech helped save his political career. It became known as the "Checkers speech."

Bo and Sunny

Barack Obama (President 2009–2017)

When Barack Obama was running for president, he publicly promised his two young daughters that if he was elected, he would get them a puppy. In April 2009, after Obama had won the election, Senator Ted Kennedy presented the Obama girls with Bo, a Portuguese water dog. A second Portuguese water dog named Sunny joined the family in 2013, when she was a year old. Both dogs got to shake paws with many famous folks, including the pope.

a dog harnessed to a milkmaid's cart—a common sight in many 19th-century cities

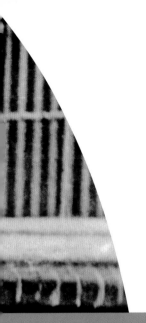

CHAPTER 6

WHO LET THE DOGS IN?

The 19th Century

In the late 18th and early 19th centuries, many people in Europe and America left their farms in the countryside and flocked to big cities in search of jobs. More and more factories sprang up during this period, which became known as the Industrial Revolution.

Dogs took jobs in cities, too. They ran alongside coaches, pulled carts, hunted vermin, operated machinery, and guarded homes and businesses. Many of those dogs led hard lives. But as a middle class began to emerge, more and more people who could afford pets began to care about the humane treatment of dogs and other animals. In fact, the laws that were passed that prevented cruelty to animals paved the way for later laws that prevented cruelty to children.

Dogs and priests rescuing an injured skier near the Great Saint Bernard pass

Saint Bernards to the Rescue

The Great Saint Bernard Pass is a 50-mile (80-km)-long trek through the Alps that links Switzerland and Italy. Frequent heavy snowstorms have always made the pass extremely dangerous for travelers. A monastery was built there in 1050.

A dog's sense of smell is 1,000 to 10,000 times better than a human's, and some types of dogs are especially exceptional at searching, sniffing, and rescuing humans in trouble.

So, from the early 18th century, the monks at the monastery began training special dogs to sniff out and rescue lost travelers. These large, shaggy-coated dogs had a high tolerance for cold weather and an unusually excellent sense of direction.

The dogs traveled in threes. When they found a stranded traveler, two would stay with the person while the third ran for help. Sometimes the dogs would dig through the snow and lie on top of an injured person to keep him warm. They probably saved thousands of lives. They were called Alpine dogs, Alpine mastiffs, mountain dogs, and many other names. It wasn't until 1880 that the Swiss Kennel Club finally recognized the breed and officially called it the Saint Bernard. Nowadays the monks rely mostly on helicopters to rescue people.

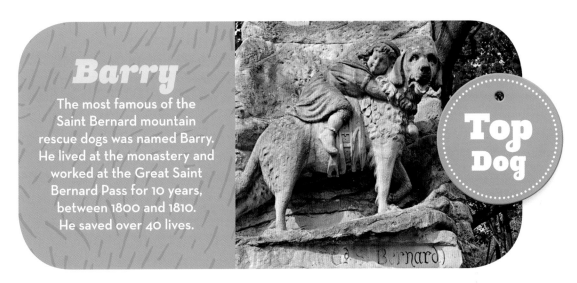

Barry

The most famous of the Saint Bernard mountain rescue dogs was named Barry. He lived at the monastery and worked at the Great Saint Bernard Pass for 10 years, between 1800 and 1810. He saved over 40 lives.

Top Dog

Lewis and Clark's Explorer Dog

In 1803, President Thomas Jefferson sent Meriwether Lewis and William Clark to explore the newly purchased Louisiana territory. Their mission was to explore the uncharted west, all the way to the Pacific Ocean. Lewis purchased a "dogge of the newfoundland breed" for the trip, which began in August 1803, and was to last for four years. The dog, Seaman, is mentioned often in Clark's journals. Clark was a terrible speller. He also had terrible handwriting. So for a long time historians thought the dog's name was "Scannon." Besides acting as guard and companion, Seaman caught squirrels for the explorers' meals and retrieved game they had shot for food. He was also an excellent swimmer. A year into the trip, he was bitten by a beaver in the hind leg. He nearly bled to death, but recovered. Later in the trip, a huge buffalo charged into the camp, heading straight toward a tent. Seaman leapt into the animal's path, snarling and barking, and caused it to change direction.

a statue of Lewis (right) and Clark (left) with Seaman, at a park in St. Charles, Missouri

The Emperor Strikes Back

Napoleon and Josephine Bonaparte were crowned emperor and empress of France in 1804. Even 10 years earlier, no one—probably not even Napoleon and Josephine—would have predicted this would happen. Napoleon had risen rapidly from his position as an obscure artillery officer, and Josephine had been in prison on the brink of being put to death.

Josephine had been married to someone else before Napoleon. His name was Alexandre, Viscount de Beauharnais. They had two children together. Alexandre had been a member of the French nobility. This was not a healthy thing to be during the French Revolution.

In 1794, during the French Revolution's Reign of Terror, many members of the upper class were arrested and killed. Josephine and her husband were imprisoned. Alexandre was sent to the guillotine. Josephine seemed headed for the same fate. While in prison, Josephine was forbidden from writing letters, but she was permitted visits from her little dog, a pug called Fortuné. She managed to send and receive notes from her children, concealed in the dog's collar. Three days after Josephine's husband's execution, the leader of the Terror, Robespierre, was himself executed. Josephine was released from prison.

In 1796, she married Napoleon Bonaparte. Napoleon became the leader of France after the Revolution.

Napoleon hated dogs. On their wedding night, Josephine refused to remove Fortuné from the bed. Fortuné bit Napoleon in the calf. But later, in one of his many love letters to Josephine, Napoleon grudgingly ended with,

Millions of kisses, some even to Fortuné, in spite of his naughtiness.

Sadly for Fortuné, the little dog met his end in a fight with the cook's bulldog. Josephine replaced him with a new pug, over protests from Napoleon. When the cook later apologized to Napoleon and assured him that the bulldog had been sent away, Napoleon supposedly said, "Bring him back. Perhaps he will rid me of the new dog too."

A glowering Napoleon. Perhaps he was thinking about Fortuné.

64

 In a painting entitled "Sympathy," the expression of this faithful dog that has joined its young human in her time-out helps dramatize the situation.

Pooches in Paintings

If the 18th century was notable for its art devoted to fancy pooch portraiture, the 19th century sparked a new trend in painting: using dogs to represent the human condition. Some artists used dogs to comment on social problems by painting plump, pampered pets next to starving street dogs. Others painted dogs with very human-looking emotions on their dog faces. Still others used dogs to show an idealized view of the lives of working people: happy, healthy children from the countryside with their loving, faithful dogs. This ideal was generally far from what real working people's lives looked like, but these paintings were meant to hang on the walls of the well-to-do.

Harnessing Dog Power

In the early 1800s, the Saturday markets in many large cities were clogged with dog carts. In London, New York, Brussels, and Amsterdam, dogs pulled carts full of market wares and water through narrow city streets. The cart dogs were also handy for guarding the wares while the master was making a delivery. The dogs toiled alongside horses and donkeys, also pulling carts.

Life for working people wasn't easy, and it was no better for their animals. In many poor neighborhoods, horses and dogs fell down dead as they worked. By the 1830s, there were movements to ban using dogs to pull heavy loads. While some people were concerned about the dogs, other people were more concerned that making them thirsty might give them rabies. (See page 55.)

The first country to ban dog carts was England, in 1855. Around the same time, New York passed similar laws, but did not ban them completely. In the 1870s, there was also a move in New York to ban dog treadmills like those that turned spits and cider presses. But that ban was not strictly enforced, either. In most busy urban centers of the 19th century, dogs continued to be used to churn butter, press fruit, pump water, grind grain, and even power sewing machines.

 large cart dogs pulling a passenger cart in Antwerp, Belgium, about 1898

 Queen Victoria and her husband, Prince Albert, were big dog fans.

Preventing Cruelty:
The RSPCA and the ASPCA

A rising interest in animal rights and preventing the mistreatment of animals began in the early 1800s. In England, the Society for the Prevention of Cruelty to Animals (SPCA) was created in 1824. In 1840 Queen Victoria gave permission to add "Royal" to the name, so it became the RSPCA.

In 1866, an American philanthropist named Henry Bergh created the American Society for the Prevention of Cruelty to Animals (ASPCA). Nine days later, the first anti-cruelty law was passed that allowed the ASPCA to investigate complaints and make arrests in cases of animal cruelty. Kinder treatment of animals probably caused the public to consider the kinder treatment of children. Eight years later, the New York Society for the Prevention of Cruelty to Children was established.

Dogs on Display

In England, the first formal British dog show was held in 1859. Just two kinds of dogs were featured: pointers and setters, both hunting dogs. But dog shows proved so popular, more shows were put on that included a larger variety of breeds.

The Kennel Club, a British group that officially recognizes purebred dogs, was established in 1873. French and Italian Kennel Clubs were established in 1882, and a year later, the American Kennel Club was formed.

Before the middle of the century, two dogs from the same breed might look quite different from one another. But with the establishment of the kennel clubs and their rules, breeds were required to look more standardized.

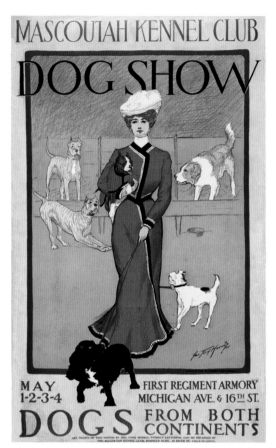

MASCOUTAH KENNEL CLUB
DOG SHOW
MAY 1-2-3-4
FIRST REGIMENT ARMORY
MICHIGAN AVE. & 16TH ST.
DOGS FROM BOTH CONTINENTS

 a poster advertising an American dog show

Paws to Consider

By the end of the 19th century, a fancy purebred dog could sell for close to $100,000 in today's money. A new kind of crime arose. Purebred dogs were dognapped and turned in at the dog shelters for 50 cents apiece. Other criminals returned the "lost" dogs to their owners and collected rewards.

Getting Sniffy

As the 19th century wore on, new inventions and better methods of producing goods and services led to the rise of a larger middle class. This new group of people had more money to spend. Many wanted fancy dogs to advertise their wealth. Purebred dogs became big status symbols. Grocery stores displayed dog-related products for grooming, health, and treats. By the middle of the century, the frenzy for breeding dogs reached a new high. More and more dogs moved inside and became part of the family.

It was also an extremely prejudiced time. Slavery was not abolished in England until 1833. In the United States it remained legal until 1865. Class-conscious people believed it was wrong to marry someone outside one's social class or heritage. They believed that lower-income people were naturally inferior to "higher-born" people. The same thinking held true for dogs. Many cities waged war on "mongrels," dogs that were not recognizable breeds. The divide between dogs owned by the wealthy and those owned by the working classes widened. Wealthier people associated purebred dogs with higher morals.

In an 1891 book called *Man's Friend, the Dog*, the author wrote, "No one would plant weeds in a flower garden. Why have mongrels as pets?"

In this 19th-century portrait, a famous actress, Sarah Bernhardt, lounges in luxury with her fancy dog.

The First Commercial Pet Food

Besides fancy leashes, collars, and beds, a new 19th-century product was introduced: pet food.

For most of history, dogs ate whatever their owners could afford to feed them. For most dogs belonging to working people, that meant not very high-quality food. Turnspit dogs were lucky to get a crust of bread. Even in better-off homes, pet dogs were fed table scraps. As the number of pet dogs (and cats) in cities increased, some enterprising manufacturers began carting away horses that had died of old age or over-work, and turned them into pet food. Something had to be done.

In the mid-1800s, an American electrician and lightning rod salesman named James Spratt visited London. At the waterfront, Spratt noticed some stray dogs gnawing on hardtack. Hardtack was a rock-hard biscuit made from flour and water. For centuries, it had been a standard and much hated food for soldiers and sailors, useful because it never spoiled. The hardtack gave Spratt an idea: biscuits for dogs. He called his new product Spratt's Patent Meat Fibrine Dog Cakes, and it became the first commercially available food for dogs. Back in America, he ran ads that convinced consumers that table scraps were no longer desirable pet food. Canned pet food appeared around 1910. When meat was rationed during World War I (1914–1918), more and more people fed their pets dry food. By the end of World War II, when many households were looking for convenience, the demand for commercial pet food skyrocketed.

Paws to Consider

Nowadays, Americans spend more than five billion dollars a year on dog food.

Lion Dogs

From as far back as 1000 B.C., all the way through to the mid-1800s, only Chinese royalty owned Pekinese dogs (see page 29). The dogs were bathed in perfume and carried on silk cushions. Their very existence was a highly protected secret. Servants and delivery people were commanded to avert their eyes when they passed one of these royal dogs.

Looty, a Pekinese lion dog

That all changed in 1860, during a conflict between China and Great Britain known as the Opium Wars. British and French soldiers stormed the Chinese summer palace, which the empress had hastily abandoned. The soldiers discovered several abandoned Pekinese dogs. Some of the dogs were carried off by soldiers, and others were probably taken by palace servants. The secret of these dogs was out.

In 1861, a British captain brought one of the dogs from Peking (now Beijing) back to England. He presented the dog to Queen Victoria of England. It was given the name "Looty." By 1890, interest in Pekinese dogs was growing in England, but only female dogs seemed to have made it west. One day, Lady Algernon Gordon-Lennox happened to glimpse a pair of "Pekes" walking through a park, and one was clearly male. Racing after the owner, she arranged to have the male dog mate with her female. The chance encounter ensured that Pekinese dogs survived, and they became a status symbol among wealthy British aristocrats, along with poodles and King Charles spaniels.

In 1911, the Chinese Qing dynasty was overthrown, and Pekinese dogs fell out of favor in China. They were seen as symbols of the old aristocracy. By the 1960s, the breed was almost completely wiped out in China. Modern-day Pekinese have managed a comeback. In 2012, a Pekinese won Best in Show at the Westminster Kennel Club Dog Show.

Rabies Remedy

On a hot July morning in 1885, a frantic mother dragged her feverish child through the streets of Paris. She was searching for someone, a scientist she had never met, named Louis Pasteur. Her child, nine-year-old Joseph Meister, had been viciously bitten in 14 places by a rabid dog, and she had heard a rumor that Pasteur had developed a treatment for rabies. She met a young doctor in a hospital who knew Pasteur, and he took her and Joseph straight to Pasteur's laboratory.

A chemist and inventor, Louis Pasteur (1822–1895) may be best remembered as the person who figured out how to keep milk from spoiling through the process of pasteurization, which bears his name. But he did so much more. His research into germs and microscopic bacteria helped scientists understand the causes of many infectious diseases, and saved untold millions of lives. It's largely thanks to him that we wash our hands before we eat, and that surgeons sterilize their instruments before they perform surgery.

He also figured out a way to prevent people from getting diseases like anthrax, cholera, tuberculosis, and smallpox, through the creation of vaccines.

Pasteur at work in his lab

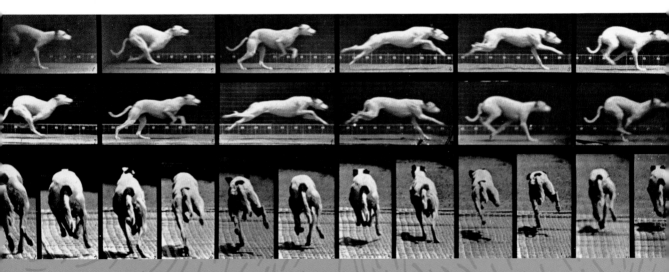

 In his amazing photos, Muybridge proved that running dogs (and racehorses) can lift all four legs off the ground at the same time.

In 1882, he focused his attention on developing a vaccine for rabies.

After examining the child, Pasteur was deeply conflicted. His vaccine had never been used on a human being, but he knew that if he did nothing, the child faced certain death. He decided to begin treating the boy. Pasteur's still-experimental method was to inject the victim every day with material from the spinal cord of a rabbit that had died of rabies. Over 10 days, the child received a total of 13 injections. Each injection contained an increasing amount of the rabies virus. The boy did not develop rabies, and lived.

Two months after that, a 15-year-old shepherd boy named Jean-Baptiste Jupille jumped in front of a rabid dog and managed to prevent it from attack-

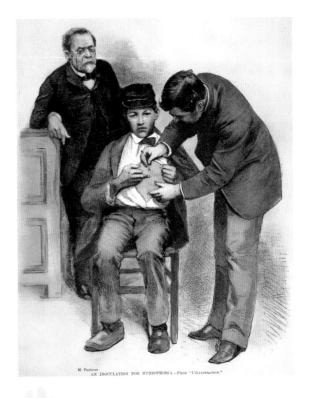

M. Pasteur.
AN INOCULATION FOR HYDROPHOBIA.—From "L'ILLUSTRATION."

Pasteur (left) oversees the treatment of nine-year-old Joseph Meister.

ing a group of younger boys. But he was severely bitten. Pasteur's vaccine worked on him as well. As word spread, hundreds of people came to see Pasteur for treatment, and over the next five years the treatment was rapidly adopted around the world.

Do the Locomotion

Dogs love to run, but their bodies are built more for endurance (energy over time) than for speed. One major exception is the greyhound. It's the fastest kind of dog, and can reach speeds of almost 37 miles an hour (60 km/h). In 1877, a British photographer named Eadweard Muybridge (1830–1904)

photographed animals (and people) in motion. His dog images featured a running greyhound. His images captured the dog's movements frame by frame, fractions of a second apart. They showed scientists and artists, for the first time, a close-up view of how dogs bend their legs and move their bodies in space.

A sleek and fancy dog in a 1929 magazine helps advertise sleek and fancy products for the wealthy.

CHAPTER 7

AD DOGS, GLAD DOGS, SAD DOGS, AND FAD DOGS

The Early 20th Century

As the world moved into the modern era, dogs' roles expanded. Dogs reported for duty on both sides of the conflict in World War I. They accompanied explorers to every corner of the world. Fancy dogs were used to advertise fancy products. A purebred dog could cost the equivalent of what a modern-day high-end sports car might cost today. Twentieth-century dogs starred in movies, kept company with world leaders, and risked their lives to save those of others.

North Pole Rivals

In August 1908, Robert Peary and Matthew Henson, along with several dozen other men, departed New York for Greenland on a ship called the *Roosevelt*. Their goal was to be the first humans to reach the North Pole. The ship stopped at an island in north-west Greenland. Thirty-nine Inuit men and women and over 200 Inuit dogs joined the expedition. The dogs were mostly huskies. Huskies have a thick double coat and are well suited for the brutal North Pole climate.

The explorer Matthew Henson holding an arctic musk ox. One of his dogs rests in the snow behind him.

The last part of the journey began in February 1909. Twenty-four men, 19 sleds, and 133 dogs began the trek to the pole. Along the way each dog was fed one pound (.45 kg) per day of pemmican, a mixture of dried ground meat, animal fat, and raisins. The farther north the travelers went, the more they lightened their load, sending people, supplies, and dogs back to the base camp.

By April 6, 1909, there were only six people left: Peary, Henson, and four native men named Ootah, Egingwah, Seegloo, and Ooqueah. They were down to five sleds and 40 of the healthiest dogs. They planted a flag at what they thought was the North Pole (although some modern scientists estimate they may have been off by 30 to 60 miles [50 to 100 km]).

When Peary and Henson returned to the ship waiting for them in northwest Greenland, they were devastated to learn that another American explorer named Frederick Cook claimed to have reached the North Pole a year earlier. After a congressional inquiry, Cook's account was deemed untruthful, and Peary (who was white) was declared the first man to reach the pole.

Because of the racial prejudice of the time, neither Peary's co-explorer, Matthew Henson (who was black), nor any of the four native men were given credit. (Many years later, the contributions of Henson were finally acknowledged and he was elected into the Explorers Club.) To this day, it's not certain which of the exploring parties—Cook's or Peary's—reached the North Pole first or if, in fact, either actually did. One thing's for certain: None of them could have done it without the dogs.

South Pole Saga

In 1910, another race to be the first to reach the pole began. This time it was to the South Pole. One of the teams was led by a Norwegian, Roald Amundsen. The other was led by his rival, an Englishman named Robert Scott. Each embarked on the treacherous 1,800-mile (2,900-km) trek across Antarctica using very different tactics. Scott brought a few dogs, but he chose to rely largely on motorized sleds and ponies. In contrast, Amundsen brought strong, well-trained dogs to pull his sledges.

The crew of Roald Amundsen sets up a camp en route to the South Pole.

Scott's motorized vehicles broke down early in the journey. The ponies tired quickly and their hooves sank into the snow. To make matters worse, he and his men did not have the proper clothing for the journey. On top of that, Scott was uncomfortable using dogs the way Amundsen did. Amundsen used some of his dogs for food along the way.

Amundsen reached the South Pole on December 15, 1911. For the final leg of the journey, he had set out with 52 huskies. The dogs ate seal meat and blubber. As rations got leaner, some of the dogs were killed and eaten. Only 11 of his dogs returned.

Scott and four companions reached the pole a month after Amundsen had, and Amundsen's flags were already flying when the British team got there. Scott and his team did not make it back alive. They died of starvation and exposure.

Inuit Dogs

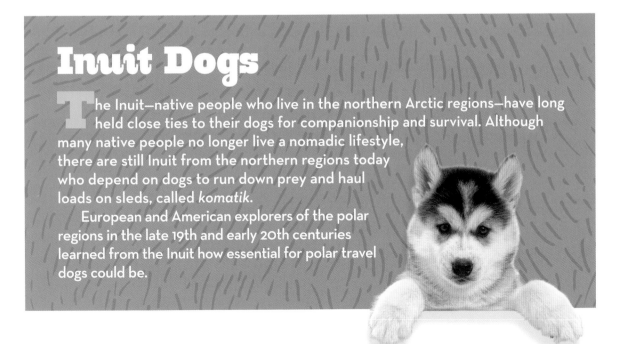

The Inuit—native people who live in the northern Arctic regions—have long held close ties to their dogs for companionship and survival. Although many native people no longer live a nomadic lifestyle, there are still Inuit from the northern regions today who depend on dogs to run down prey and haul loads on sleds, called *komatik*.

European and American explorers of the polar regions in the late 19th and early 20th centuries learned from the Inuit how essential for polar travel dogs could be.

World War I Dogs

At the beginning of the 20th century, as tensions rose among rival nations, Germany began a campaign to strengthen its military power. As part of this plan, the Germans established several military dog-training schools. By the time World War I began, in 1914, the Germans had trained as many as 30,000 dogs for military service, and the number increased to nearly 48,000 by the time the war ended in 1918. German dogs hauled weapons and supplies, carried messages, and helped seek out wounded soldiers on the battlefield.

The countries on the opposing side, known as the Allies (primarily Great Britain, France, Russia, and Italy) scrambled to catch up to the Germans' dog-force. They established doggie boot camps—war dog schools—in France, Italy, Belgium, and England. Three years later, in 1917, the United States entered the war on the side of the Allies. The Americans had no dog-training schools at the time, so they had to borrow dogs from their allies.

Allied dogs played many roles. Irish wolfhounds were trained to chase down enemy messengers and knock them off their bicycles. Greyhounds, with their excellent sight, were trained to bark an alarm at the first sign of enemy movements. Ambulance dogs pulled wounded soldiers on two-wheeled carriers. Red Cross dogs were trained to find wounded soldiers on the battlefield and then lead stretcher bearers to the scene.

One French Red Cross dog named Prusco located more than a hundred wounded men after a single battle. The large dog managed to drag wounded and unconscious soldiers into trenches and craters to keep them safe before running back for help.

Terriers were used to hunt and destroy rats that swarmed through the muddy trenches.

For American troops, several dogs served as mascots—that meant they didn't have special training, and were just there for comfort and friendship. But many of these dogs ended up performing heroic feats. (See Stubby, opposite.)

a British soldier and his canine friend, from about 1914

Political Pooches

When World War I broke out and Allied powers went to war against Germany, the dachshund became a symbol of Germany in political cartoons and anti-German war posters. Because of anti-German sentiments in America, the American Kennel Club officially renamed it the "badger dog," while others called it a "liberty pup." The German shepherd was renamed the Alsatian for the same reason. People stopped calling hot dogs "frankfurters" so that the popular food would not be associated with the city of Frankfurt, Germany.

Although the dachshund would be associated with Germany through another war (World War II), it has remained a popular pet in America.

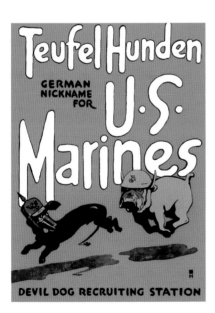

The German "Teufel Hunden" refers to fierce dogs from German folktales.

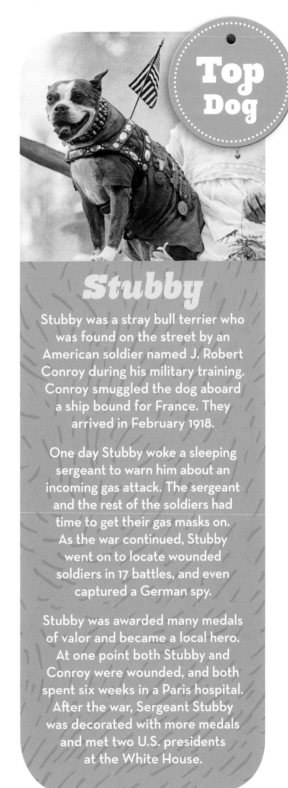

Stubby

Stubby was a stray bull terrier who was found on the street by an American soldier named J. Robert Conroy during his military training. Conroy smuggled the dog aboard a ship bound for France. They arrived in February 1918.

One day Stubby woke a sleeping sergeant to warn him about an incoming gas attack. The sergeant and the rest of the soldiers had time to get their gas masks on. As the war continued, Stubby went on to locate wounded soldiers in 17 battles, and even captured a German spy.

Stubby was awarded many medals of valor and became a local hero. At one point both Stubby and Conroy were wounded, and both spent six weeks in a Paris hospital. After the war, Sergeant Stubby was decorated with more medals and met two U.S. presidents at the White House.

🐾 Running for Their Lives ··

In December 1924, a two-year-old Inuit boy living in the town of Nome, Alaska, fell seriously ill. It turned out that the child had a dreaded, highly contagious disease called diphtheria (dif-THEER-e-uh), but the doctor misdiagnosed it as tonsillitis. The child died. Two more children with similar symptoms also died. It wasn't until January 20, 1925, that the first case of diphtheria was properly diagnosed. Several more cases followed. On January 24, doctors at the hospital sent an urgent telegram to the U.S. Public Health Service in Washington, D.C., with a desperate call for a life-saving medication, known as an antitoxin serum. The serum could save the lives of close to 300 exposed patients, many of them children.

🐾 **Togo and his team, with their driver, Leonhard Seppala**

An urgent meeting was held in Washington, D.C. Should they try to get the serum to Nome by airplane, or by train and then dogsled? Authorities decided that flying was too risky under the brutal weather conditions. The serum would be delivered by a team of dogsleds, pulled by Siberian huskies. The first team would leave from a town called Nenana, which was the end of the line for the railway.

Balto, now famous, posing for a picture with a well-known child actor in Hollywood

On January 27, the governor of Alaska gave final authorization for the dogsled relay. There would be 19 teams of the best drivers and dogs, and they would race through the interior of the territory with its howling winds, where temperatures plunged as low as 70 degrees below zero Fahrenheit (-57°C). The package of medicine weighed about 20 pounds (9 kg). The crisis became headline news. The world watched and listened as newspapers and radios reported breathlessly about the desperate 674-mile (1,085-km) race. On one leg of the journey, the famous 12-year-old dog, Togo, led his team across a dangerous, icy part of Norton Sound, covering 84 miles (135 km) in one day. After resting briefly, Togo's team set out again at 2 a.m., into a howling storm. They toiled up a 5,000-foot (8,050-km) mountain before reaching the next post and delivering the medicine to the next team. Led by the driver, Leonhard Seppala, Togo and his team ran nearly five times as far as any of the other 18 teams (about 261 miles [420 km]).

For the final leg of the journey, a man named Gunnar Kaasen set out early on the morning of February 1 with a team led by a dog named Balto. Visibility was so poor, Kaasen couldn't even see his closest dogs. At one point the sled flipped over, and Kaasen nearly lost the package of medicine. He dug for it with his bare hands and finally found it, but suffered severe frostbite.

Kaasen, Balto, and the rest of the team arrived in Nome at 5:30 a.m., five days after the first team had begun. They delivered the lifesaving medicine.

Three years later, a businessman from Cleveland, Ohio, was shocked to discover that Balto and his team had been sold to a cheap carnival show in Los Angeles. The dogs were living in dismal conditions. He created a major fund-raising event, and the dogs were purchased for $2,300 and brought to Cleveland. There they met with a hero's reception and spent the remainder of their lives in comfort at the Cleveland Brookside Zoo.

Top Dog

Hachiko

A professor at the University of Tokyo (in Japan) named Eisaburo Ueno owned a dog named Hachiko. Hachiko was a breed called an Akita. Every day at 3 p.m., Hachiko ran to the train station platform to greet his master and walk him home. One day, the professor didn't return. He had died suddenly at work. For the next 11 years, Hachiko kept returning to the station to wait for his master. When Hachiko finally died in 1935, a statue was raised in his honor. The Akita is now the national breed of Japan.

A guide dog's stiff harness helps the blind person feel the dog's movements.

Seeing Eye Dogs

In 1927, a guide dog program in Germany began training dogs to help World War I veterans who had been blinded in the war by poisonous gas. An American named Dorothy Harrison Eustis trained German shepherds at a similar program in Switzerland. A blind American named Morris Frank heard about the program and wrote to her. He asked her for help in getting his own trained dog. She agreed, and he flew to Switzerland to work with her in training a dog. Frank returned with a female German shepherd named Buddy, who became the first dog in America to be formally trained to assist the blind. Frank and Eustis cofounded the Seeing Eye school, the first of its kind in America, and in February 1929, the first class of dogs graduated.

Analyze This: Freud's Dog

The famed psychoanalyst Sigmund Freud [pronounced FROYD] had a Chinese chow breed of dog named Yofi, who stayed in Freud's office during sessions with patients. He claimed she helped him assess patients. If a person was full of tension, Yofi moved away. If the person was calm, Yofi sat close enough to be patted. She also had an excellent sense of timing—she knew how long a session should last. When 50 minutes were up, she yawned, so Freud didn't have to look at his watch.

Freud's dog, Yofi, showing her expressive face

Paws to Consider

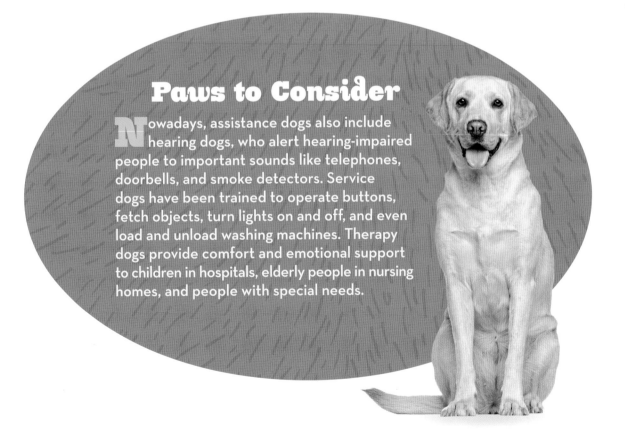

Nowadays, assistance dogs also include hearing dogs, who alert hearing-impaired people to important sounds like telephones, doorbells, and smoke detectors. Service dogs have been trained to operate buttons, fetch objects, turn lights on and off, and even load and unload washing machines. Therapy dogs provide comfort and emotional support to children in hospitals, elderly people in nursing homes, and people with special needs.

🐾 Reel-Life Dog ················

Rover

In 1905, in the earliest days of "moving pictures," a British man named Cecil M. Hepworth produced a six-minute film called *Rescued by Rover*. In the not-very-complicated plot, a baby was kidnapped, and then rescued by Rover. Rover was a dog. Hepworth played the distraught father, his wife, the distraught mother, and their infant daughter, Elizabeth, the baby. The family dog, Blair, played the part of Rover. Moviemaking special effects were still very new in 1905, but Hepworth made it look as though Rover were driving a car all by himself. The movie was a hit, and so was the riveting sequel, *The Dog Outwits the Kidnapper*. After the movies were released, the name "Rover" became popular among dog owners.

Ad Dog 🐾 ·····················

Nipper

Sometime in the 1890s, a painter named Francis Barraud painted a portrait of his brother's dog. The dog was named Nipper. In the original painting, Nipper sat with his head slightly cocked. He seemed to be listening to a phonograph. The phonograph had just been invented by Thomas Edison, and was used to record or play sounds.

In 1900, the Gramophone Company bought the painting from Barraud, and asked him to change the phonograph to a gramophone (a somewhat later kind of device that played sounds on a flat, spinning disk). The Victor Talking Machine Company used the painting as a trademark in 1902. The Gramophone Company used it in 1909. It's one of the most recognized trademark pictures in history.

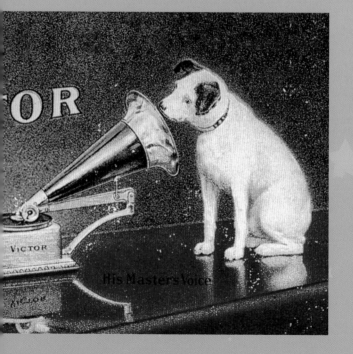

His Master's Voice

🐾 Showbiz Dog ······················

Rin Tin Tin

On September 15, 1918, at the very end of World War I, a U.S. corporal named Lee Duncan rescued two puppies from a bombed-out kennel in France. One of them got sick and died. Duncan named the other one Rin Tin Tin, and brought him home to Los Angeles.

Duncan spent many hours training "Rinty," and dreamed of landing the dog a role in a film. And then one day they got their lucky break. A film crew happened to be in the neighborhood and Duncan observed them trying to film a scene with a "wolf." The dog actor was not cooperating. Duncan offered his dog, and Rin Tin Tin nailed the scene. He would go on to star in 26 movies. He even had his own chef and chauffeur.

Dorothy's Dog 🐾 ···········

Terry the Terrier

A female Cairn terrier named Terry starred in 16 movies, but her most famous role was playing Toto, Dorothy's pet dog, in the 1939 movie *The Wizard of Oz*. She also costarred in a movie called *Bright Eyes*, with the child-star Shirley Temple.

🐾 Literary Dog ·················

Luath

The Scottish novelist and playwright J. M. Barrie is best known for creating the character Peter Pan. In that story, the fictional dog-nanny character, Nana, takes care of the Darling children. Nana the dog was based on Barrie's real-life pet Newfoundland named Luath.

a 1950s American Dream:
a house, a car, and a family dog

CHAPTER 8

WAR DOGS AND COLD WAR DOGS

Moving Into Modern Times

As the 20th century unfolded, economic turmoil and unstable governments gave rise to cruel dictators intent on seizing more power and expanding territories. In 1939, the world went to war once again. Dogs played a crucial role during World War II, on both sides. After the war ended, in 1945, a new period of tension began between democratic countries in the Western world and communist countries of Eastern Europe. Relations were especially strained between the Soviet Union and the United States. That postwar unease between the two superpowers became known as the Cold War. Dogs played a vital role in the Cold War as well, all the way up to the end of the American war in Vietnam.

 In 1941 London, a dog assists
rescue teams searching for
victims after a German bombing attack.

World War II Dogs

In 1939, Adolf Hitler's German army invaded Poland. Poland's allies, France and
Britain, declared war on Germany, and the Second World War began. In 1941, Germany
invaded the Soviet Union, and Japan attacked the American naval base at Pearl
Harbor, near Honolulu, Hawaii. America and the Soviet Union also entered the war,
siding with France and Britain and the rest of the Allied powers.

a mascot dog aboard a U.S.
Navy ship in the Sea of Japan

Germany employed as many as
200,000 dogs during the war. The
Japanese had about 25,000, and the
Soviet Union about 50,000. Russian
dogs were trained to sniff out land mines
(buried explosive devices). One mixed-
breed dog named Zucha discovered
2,000 buried explosives in less than two
weeks. The Soviets trained other dogs
to sneak into enemy outposts and steal
maps and other documents. Still others
were strapped with explosives and
trained to run underneath enemy tanks.

Meanwhile, the city of London was repeatedly bombed by Germany in what is known as the Blitz. British-trained dogs sniffed out victims in the rubble of bomb sites.

In battles that took place around the Pacific Ocean, the U.S. Marines trained a troop of Doberman pinschers to capture enemies and to alert soldiers of the existence of enemy ambushes. The American dog troop was called the "Devil Dogs." American marines were also nicknamed Devil Dogs.

In 1942, the American military recruited dogs for service through a civilian agency called Dogs for Defense. Many families "enlisted" their pet dogs in service to the country.

World War II American fighter pilots pose with their two mascots—a dog and a monkey.

Chips

Chips was a mixed-breed dog who was one of more than 10,000 dogs trained by the U.S. K-9 Corps in World War II. He was trained as a scout dog for the U.S. Army and was a member of the first War Dog Detachment that got sent overseas, in 1942. In 1943 he was one of three dogs that stood guard for a meeting between the U.S. president Franklin D. Roosevelt and the British prime minister Winston Churchill.

Another day in 1943, Chips broke away from his handler and flung himself into what looked like an abandoned guard post, called a "pill box." It turned out not to be empty—it held four enemy soldiers. Chips was wounded in that encounter, but survived, and later received a Purple Heart and a Silver Star. He almost bit General Eisenhower when receiving his medals.

Canine Cosmonauts

The 1950s in America were notable for many things, including the rise of a prosperous white middle class, harsh racial discrimination, and anti-communist sentiment. The theory behind a communist form of government is that wealth is shared equally among everyone. In postwar Soviet Union, the reality was that the Communist Party allowed its citizens few rights or freedoms. Another feature of the 1950s? More and more American families owned television sets.

It was the height of the Cold War, and a fierce competition arose between the Americans and the Russians: Who would be the first to launch a spaceship into orbit? Who would be the first to send astronauts to the moon?

On November 3, 1957, in a rush to be the first, the Russians launched a Sputnik satellite into orbit. No humans were on board, but someone else was: a dog named Laika. The orbit was successful.

Laika, a mixed-breed street dog from Moscow, was scornfully nicknamed "Muttnik" in the American press. The mission outraged people in America, who had watched the

Dogs in Songs

The four members of the wildly popular British rock group, the Beatles, were dog lovers. At the end of their song "A Day in the Life" (1967), the band put in a dog whistle, which is barely audible to humans but which dogs are able to hear.

Also, the song "Martha My Dear" (1968) is about Paul McCartney's beloved sheepdog.

 Martha and Paul McCartney

news on their new televisions. Most Americans had assumed that their technology was superior to that of the Russians. Also, the Russians hadn't yet figured out how to get the satellite back to Earth, so Laika did not survive the trip.

Then three years later, on August 19, 1960, the Soviet Union launched another spaceship, Sputnik 5. This time there were two dogs on board, named Strelka and Belka. By now the Russians had improved the technology. Strelka and Belka boarded the spacecraft along with 40 mice, two rats, and some plants—and they orbited the Earth for 16 hours before returning back home. That made them the first living creatures to return safely after an orbital flight. The dogs—both of them mutts—had been through rigorous training to prepare for their flight. They got used to wearing a space suit. Because they would have to sit still for the entire flight, their training involved being confined in smaller and smaller boxes and exposed to flight simulators for hours on end.

Strelka and Belka's flight occurred just two months before the American presidential election. John F. Kennedy won, in part because he had promised that if he got elected, he would send an American to the moon by the end of the decade. The president would not live to see his promise fulfilled. He was assassinated in 1963. But Americans did make it to the moon first, in 1969.

**Belka (left)
and Strelka (right)
after their return from space**

Sentries and Scouts

War dogs played an important role during the American war in Vietnam (1963-1975). America's decision to enter the conflict in Vietnam was a direct result of the Cold War between the U.S. and the U.S.S.R. When Communist-controlled North Vietnam began a war against South Vietnam in 1963, many Americans believed that Communism was threatening to expand all over Southeast Asia. As many as 4,000 dogs

An American soldier and his dog cool off in a stream near Saigon, South Vietnam, in 1967.

provided sentry and scout duty to Americans and their allies in South Vietnam. The dogs, mostly German shepherds and Labrador retrievers, scouted out booby traps, ambushes, and enemy fighters. The dogs in Vietnam saved thousands of soldiers' lives.

Ironically, dogs performed a different role back in the United States. Anti-war protests and riots raged across the country, and police often used dogs to control the crowds of demonstrators.

In a tragic footnote to a tragic chapter in history, South Vietnam fell to the North Vietnamese in 1975, and many dogs were left behind in the frantic scramble to evacuate Americans. The dogs were looked on by the American military as "surplus equipment."

That policy changed in the year 2000. President Bill Clinton signed a new law. No longer would military working dogs (MWDs) be left behind during wartime. Also, military dogs could now be adopted. The handlers would be given the first option, but other qualified applicants would also be allowed.

Bottom left: American troops board a plane with their scout dog in Vietnam, 1967. Bottom right: An American soldier patrols with his dog in Vietnam.

Well-fed, well-groomed, and well-trained—but have we created genetic problems for this little "sausage dog"?

CHAPTER 9

NICE WORK

Present-Day Dogs, Future Challenges

Basic "types" of dogs—war dogs, sight dogs, scent dogs, working dogs, and toy dogs—have been around since ancient times. But breeds, as we think of them in the modern sense, are a relatively recent development. Have we taken things too far?

No matter whether they're purebred or mixed breeds, our attachment to our dogs is deepening. We can now buy organic, grain-free, non-genetically-modified dog food that contains choice cuts of meat, poultry, and fish. That fancy food accounts for more than 40 percent of dog food sales. Whether or not our elaborate spending is good for our dogs, our dogs continue to prove that they're good for us.

Survival of the Unfittest

The creation of kennel clubs in the 19th century marked the start of the general public's fascination with purebred dogs. But 19th-century dog breeds were judged not only for their looks, but also for various behaviors and physical abilities.

With their smooshed snouts and folds of fur, many modern bulldogs suffer from breathing and skin problems.

Only very recently—in the past few decades—have many dogs been bred solely for the way they look. Their physical appearance must strictly conform to the standards that have been specified by breed-specific dog clubs, and by the American Kennel Club and its European kennel club counterparts. As a result of this focus on looking good, as many as one in four purebred dogs is a medical mess. We may have over-engineered dogs, just to suit our human purposes. To emphasize certain desired traits, breeders mate dogs that are too closely related. This kind of inbreeding can cause dangerous genetic problems.

Today there are many examples of physical and behavioral problems that happen when breeders take things too far. Certain breeds now have snouts that are too flat for the dogs to breathe properly, eyes that are too large for their faces, legs too short for their bodies, or hips too

Paws to Consider

Today there is a huge market for luxury toys, food, and beds for dogs. There are dog bakeries, high-end kennels, doggy day care, dog exercise treadmills, doggie nail "pawlish," gold-embossed dog dishes, and even doggie tiaras. In the United States, the average dog owner spends over $1,500 a year on pet-related stuff.

 **Many modern German shepherds suffer from joint and hip problems.**

sloped to walk and run without pain. Some breeds even have brains that grow too large for their skulls. Many other breeds, once prized for their intelligence and ability to learn quickly, can no longer be used for service or police work.

The huge public demand for pure-bred dogs has led to another unfortunate industry: puppy mills. These are big, commercial dog-breeding facilities that tend to sell to pet stores and that don't treat their dogs well.

Recently there have been encouraging signs that some of the standard breed requirements are starting to loosen up a bit, to take into account not just the dog's good looks, but also its health. And in 2009, the American Kennel Club permitted mixed breeds (mutts) to participate in its agility contest.

Fetching Names

Today's most popular dog names:

Bella

Lucy

Max

Daisy

Bailey

Buddy

Molly

Charlie

Maggie

Sadie

Dr. Dog

Clostridium difficile (or C. diff for short) is a contagious and potentially life-threatening human disease. It's also complicated to diagnose—a doctor may not realize the patient has it immediately, and the test for it can take one to two days for confirmation. By that time, the disease may have spread.

In 2012, a beagle named Cliff was trained to sniff C. diff. Cliff was taken around two Dutch teaching hospitals to try to detect it in patients. He was led around the wards by his trainer, who had no idea which patients had C. diff and which ones did not. There was one sick patient out of every ten. He had been taught to sit or lie down when he detected C. diff. He correctly identified 25 out of every 30 cases.

As it turns out, cancer cells also produce distinctive odors, and if you're a dog you can be trained to recognize the smell. Humans have about 5 million olfactory (sniffing) cells in their noses. Dogs have about 200 million. In several published studies, trained cancer-sniffing dogs were able to sniff the breath or urine of ill patients and diagnose several kinds of cancer—often with 98 percent accuracy. That's a lot cheaper and more accurate than expensive medical tests and procedures used to diagnose the same thing.

Dogs have also been trained to help people with epilepsy and diabetes. The dogs can smell faint signals from the person who may not yet be aware of an upcoming seizure, or dangerous swings in blood sugar, while the person still has time to do something about it.

 Some dogs' sniffing skills can be more effective than many sophisticated—and expensive—medical procedures.

Top Dog

Belle

One day in February 2006, a 911 operator received a strange phone call—it was just a barking dog. An ambulance was sent, and the medics discovered that the dog's owner, Kevin Weaver, was unconscious from a diabetic seizure. His dog, a beagle named Belle, had been trained as a diabetic-alert dog. Using her nose, she knew how to alert her owner whenever his blood-sugar level was at a dangerous level, in order to avert a seizure. In case Weaver collapsed, Belle also knew how to chomp down on his cell phone—specifically the number 9— to call an ambulance. Which is exactly what she did. Weaver recovered fully, and Belle received numerous awards and medals.

The Beagle Brigade

Beagles are known for being cute, friendly, and gentle. Some of them also have jobs as federal agents. The U.S. Department of Agriculture created the dog-detective program, staffed mostly by beagles, and now run by the Department of Homeland Security. Agriculture canine teams detect fruits, vegetables, plants, and even meat products in passengers' bags and help prevent the introduction of harmful plant and animal diseases into the United States.

War Dogs of the 21st Century

There are over 3,000 dogs serving in the American military today. Dogs have saved countless American lives in Iraq and Afghanistan by sniffing out explosive devices that have been buried or hidden. They also work as service dogs for veterans suffering from post-traumatic stress disorder (PTSD).

Rosco the dog is trained to help and comfort his soldier-owner, who is suffering from the traumatic effects of war.

★ AFTERWORD ★

What Have Dogs Done for Us?

Imagine if there were a miracle cure that could make us feel better, act kinder, and live more joyfully.

Actually, there is. It's called a dog.

There are a lot of studies that show that dogs are good for us both physically and emotionally. Petting a dog or cuddling a puppy can lower a person's blood pressure, or make someone feel less anxious. Kids who grow up with a dog learn how to be kind, and how to think about another living thing besides themselves. Dogs comfort us when we're sad, keep us company when we're lonely, and share in our joy when we're happy.

It's the 21st century. Dogs still help us by herding, hunting, guarding, and sniffing out trouble. They still go to war with us. They still rescue us and comfort us. And more than ever before, they have been trained to perform highly specialized services for people who need assistance with day-to-day living.

But most important, dogs teach us about love. They love us. And we love them.

Do Owners Look Like Their Dogs?

You hear it said often enough. But just because a lot of people believe something doesn't make it true.

Two scientists, Michael M. Roy and Nicholas J. S. Christenfeld, set out to explore whether volunteers could match up pictures of dogs with pictures of the dogs' owners. Forty-five dogs and their owners were photographed separately, and people were shown an owner, an owner's dog, and one other dog. Observers were able to match owners to purebred dogs quite reliably. (The experiment had less successful results with mixed-breed dogs.) Could it be that a person chooses a dog that resembles her?

 In the 1961 Disney movie, *101 Dalmatians* (based on the book by Dodie Smith), the animators had fun with the idea that dogs look like their owners.

How Do Dogs in Other Countries Say Bow-wow?

Albanian: ham-ham

Arabic: hau-hau

Balinese: kong-kong

Bengali: gheu-gheu; bhao-bhao

Chinese-Cantonese: wo-wo; wow-wow; wong-wong

Chinese-Mandarin: wang-wang

Danish: vov-vov; vuf-vuf

Dutch: blaf-blaf; woef-woef (small dogs); kef-kef (very small dogs)

English: woof-woof; ruff-ruff; arf-arf; bow-wow; yap-yap (small dogs); yip-yip (very small dogs)

French: wouaff-wouaff; ouah-ouah; whou-whou; vaf-vaf; jappe-jappe (small dogs)

German: wuff-wuff; vow-vow

Hebrew: hav-hav; haw-haw

Hindi: bow-bow

Indonesian: guk-guk; gong-gong

Italian: bau-bau; arf-arf

Japanese: wan-wan; kian-kian

Korean: mung-mung; wang-wang

Malay: gong-gong

Nigerian (Calabar area): wai-wai

Portuguese: au-au

Russian: gav-gav; guf-guf; hav-hav; tyav-tyav (small dogs)

Spanish: guau-guau; gua-gua; jau-jau

Thai: hong-hong

Turkish: hev-hev; hav-hav

Welsh: wff-wff

A Note About the Research

Every nonfiction writer faces challenges in determining the authenticity of her sources, but researching dogs and their relationship with humans has proved to be *especially* challenging. Many dog stories that have been passed down as factual and repeated in multiple sources may in fact have been exaggerated or even fabricated.

For instance, did Napoleon, an avowed dog hater, really fall out of a boat as he was escaping from his exile on Elba and get rescued by a Newfoundland? Did King Henry VIII's minister's dog really bite the pope on the toe, enraging him enough to refuse to annul the king's marriage and thereby ushering in the Protestant Reformation? Did Alexander Pope's dog, Bounce, really bolt from her hiding place under the bed to tackle a would-be murderer of her master? They're great stories, and you can find them repeated in multiple books and Internet sites. But after a lot of careful research, I had to conclude that they probably didn't happen.

The stories that I *have* included I feel reasonably sure did happen. But it's impossible to know for certain. Stories are powerful, and facts can be slippery. The stories about extraordinary dogs that have stood the test of time may have become more and more exaggerated in the retelling.

But then again, dogs have done some extraordinary things.

Author's Note

My earliest childhood memory is when my puppy, Abby, was hit by a car. I was three years old. I remember the screech of the brakes. The distraught driver of the shiny black station wagon. Her yelps. My father rushing to the scene. He scooped her up, laid her in a cushioned box, and zoomed off to the vet with her. She survived, but the doctor had to remove one of her back legs.

We grew up together, Abby and I. My beloved three-legged dog could outrun me in a footrace. When she was three, she gave birth to a litter of seven puppies. We kept two of them—Freddie and Igor. (Igor was a girl, by the way. My older brothers named her.) Abby lived to be 15. Abby, Igor, Freddie, and Igor's son, Otis, were part of the fabric of my childhood.

Now my family has Rosie. She is an incredible dog. And she has become part of the fabric of my children's lives.

This book has been a dream to write. It was thrilling to combine two of my loves—history and dogs—and to explore what it was like to own a dog 200 or 500 or 1,000 years ago.

For starters, not so long ago—maybe when your great-grandparents were your age—most people were used to being near a *lot* more animals. People in the country usually lived around farm animals, but also frequently encountered animals from the wild—a fox trying to get into the henhouse, a wolf or coyote eyeing the sheep, a snake in the outhouse. And of course, many people had dogs.

People in cities were surrounded by horses, donkeys pulling carts, livestock driven through the streets to the market, cats, pigeons, squirrels, mice, and rats. And of course, many people had dogs.

I grew up not just with dogs, but also with cats, chickens, pigs, sheep, goats, and cows. We even had a giant, deranged watch-turkey named Simon, who chased visitors up the pathway to our front door. I feel very lucky to have known animals up close and personal. Nowadays, a dog (or perhaps a cat or a goldfish) may be the only member of the animal kingdom many kids get to know personally.

The dogs that have been part of my life have helped shape me into the person I am now. They have shown me what love looks like, and have taught me a thousand other things, big and small. I hope you are lucky enough to share your life with a dog as well.

Select Bibliography

"Agriculture Canine." U.S. Customs and Border Protection. cbp.gov/border-security/protecting-agriculture/agriculture-canine.

"Balto: The Hero Dog of Nome, Alaska." Cleveland Museum of Natural History. cmnh.org/balto.

Bausum, Ann. *Stubby the War Dog: The True Story of World War I's Bravest Dog.* Washington, D.C.: National Geographic Kids, 2014.

Beck, Melinda. "Beside Freud's Couch, a Chow Named Jofi." *Wall Street Journal*, December 21, 2010.

Blumberg, Jess. "A Brief History of the St. Bernard Rescue Dog." *Smithsonian* (March 1, 2016). smithsonianmag.com/history/a-brief-history-of-the-st-bernard-rescue-dog-13787665/?page=2.

Bomers, M. K., et al. "Using a Dog's Superior Olfactory Sensitivity to Identify *Clostridium difficile* in Stools and Patients: Proof of Principle Study." *BMJ* 345 (December 13, 2012). bmj.com/content/345/bmj.e7396.

Braun, David Maxwell. "Peary and the North Pole 100 Years Ago Today." *National Geographic Blogs*, April 6, 2009. voices.nationalgeographic.com/2009/04/06/peary_and_the_north_pole.

Breig, James. "The Eighteenth Century Goes to the Dogs." *Trend & Tradition, the Magazine of Colonial Williamsburg* (Autumn 2004). history.org/Foundation/journal/Autumn04/dogs.cfm.

Brewster, David. *The Life of Sir Isaac Newton.* archive.org/details/lifeofsirisaacne00brewrich.

Browne, Malcolm W. "Polar Exploration's Golden Age Is Still a Maker and Breaker of Reputations." *New York Times*, May 10, 1996.

Budiansky, Stephen. "Prehistoric Dog." The Truth About Dogs—99.07 (Part Two). *Atlantic Monthly* 284.1

(July 1999), 39–53. theatlantic.com/past/docs/issues/99jul/9907dogs2.htm.

Caius, John. *Of Englishe Dogges: the diuersities, the names, the natures, and the properties, 1576.* archive.org/details/englishedoggesd00flemgoog.

Castaldo, Nancy F. *Sniffer Dogs: How Dogs (and Their Noses) Save the World.* New York: Houghton Mifflin Harcourt, 2014.

Castillo, Michelle. "How Much Is That Doggy in the Window? About $60 Billion." NBC News, July 12, 2015. nbcnews.com/business/consumer/americans-will-spend-more-60-billion-their-pets-year-n390181.

Ceci, L. "Fish Fertilizer: A Native North American Practice?" *Science* 188.4183 (1975), 26–30.

"Ceramic Dogs, Colima Culture, West Mexico." Bowers Audio. Bowers Museum. bowers.org.

Cherniss, Harold, and William C. Hembold, ed. "Whether Land or Sea Animals Are Cleverer (De Sollertia Animalium)." *Perseus Digital Library.* perseus.tufts.edu/hopper/text?doc=Perseus%3Atext%3A2008.01.0369.

Church, John, et al. "Another Sniffer Dog for the Clinic?" *The Lancet* 358.9285 (September 15, 2001).

Clutton-Brock, Juliet. *Eyewitness Dog.* London: Dorling Kindersley, 2004. American edition 2014.

Cockayne, Emily. *Hubbub: Filth, Noise & Stench in England 1600–1770.* New Haven, Conn.: Yale University Press, 2007.

Coren, Stanley. "How Dogs Bark in Different Languages." *Psychology Today* (November 2012).

Coren, Stanley. *The Pawprints of History.* New York: Free Press, 2002.

Cox, Nicholas. *The gentleman's recreation: in four parts, viz., hunting, hawking, fowling, fishing: collected from ancient and modern authors forrein and domestick, and rectified by the experience of the most skilfull artists of these times : illustrated with sculptures.* Printed by E. Flesher, for Maurice Atkins ... and Nicolas Cox, London, 1962.

Craig, John. "Psalms, Groans, and Dog-Whippers: The Soundscape of Worship in the English Parish Church, 1547–1632." In *Sacred Space in Early Modern Europe*, eds. Will Coster and Andrew Spicer. Cambridge, U.K.: Cambridge University Press, 2005.

Derr, Mark. *Dog's Best Friend: Annals of the Dog-Human Relationship.* New York: Henry Holt, 1997.

Derr, Mark. *A Dog's History of America: How Our Best Friend Explored, Conquered, and Settled a Continent.* New York: North Point, 2004.

"The Diary of John Evelyn, Volume II (of 2), by John Evelyn, Edited by William Bray." *Project Gutenberg*, February 13, 2013. mirrorservice.org/sites/gutenberg.org/4/2/0/8/42081/42081-h/42081-h.htm.

Ding, Z-L, et al. "Origins of Domestic Dog in Southern East Asia Is Supported by Analysis of Y-chromosome DNA." *Heredity* 108.5 (2011), 507–14.

Donne, John. *The Flea*, 1633. poetryfoundation.org/poems-and-poets/poems/detail/46467

Duffy, Kevin. *Who Were the Celts? Everything You Ever Wanted to Know About the Celts 1000 B.C. to the Present.* New York: Barnes and Noble Books, 1999.

Evans, Jennifer. "The Biting of a Mad Dog." *Early Modern Medicine.* earlymodernmedicine.com/the-biting-of-a-mad-dog.

Fessenden, Marissa. "Humans May Have Domesticated Dogs Tens of Thousands of Years Earlier Than Thought," *Smithsonian* (May 22, 2015). smithsonianmag.com/smart-news/news/humans-may-have-domesticated-dogs-24000-years-earlier-thought-180955374.

Forbes, Esther. *Paul Revere and the World He Lived In*. Boston: Houghton Mifflin Harcourt, 1999.

Forster, E. S. "Dogs in Ancient Warfare." *Greece & Rome* 10.30 (May 1941), 114–17. jstor.org.

Frankel, Rebecca. "WDotW: Actually, No, There Are No Military Dogs Left Behind." *Foreign Policy* (September 19, 2014).

From George Washington to General William Howe, 6 October 1777. *Founders Online,* National Archives. founders.archives.gov/documents/Washington/03-11-02-0432.

Gerstenfeld, Sheldon L., and Jacque Lynne Schultz. *ASPCA Complete Guide to Dogs*. San Francisco: Chronicle Books, 1999.

Gorman, James. "Deeper Digging Needed to Decode a Best Friend's Genetic Roots." *New York Times,* May 21, 2012.

Gorrell, Gena K. *Working Like a Dog: The Story of Working Dogs Through History*. Toronto, Ontario: Tundra, 2003.

Grier, Katherine C. *Pets in America: A History*. Chapel Hill: University of North Carolina, 2006.

Grout, James, "Dogs in Rome and Greece." *Encyclopaedia Romana*. penelope.uchicago.edu/~grout/encyclopaedia_romana/miscellanea/canes/canes.html.

Hall, Alfred Rupert. *Isaac Newton: Eighteenth Century Perspectives*. New York: Oxford University Press, 1999.

Hawke, David Freeman. *Everyday Life in Early America*. New York: Harper and Row, 1988.

Hesman Saey, Tina. "Origins of Native Americans debated." *Science News* 188, no. 4 (August 22, 2015): 6–7. Academic Search Complete, EBSCOhost (accessed June 5, 2017).

Hood, Graham. "Personable Pooches." *Colonial Williamsburg Official History and Citizenship Site,* Autumn 2006. history.org/Foundation/journal/Autumn06/Dog.cfm.

Jenner, Mark S. R. "The Great Dog Massacre." In *Fear in Early Modern Society,* ed. William G. Naphy and Penny Roberts. Manchester, U.K.: Manchester University Press, 1997.

Lemish, Michael G. *War Dogs: A History of Loyalty and Heroism*. Washington, D.C.: Brassey's, 1999.

Lemonick, Michael D. "A Terrible Beauty." *Time* (December 12, 1994).

Levine, Douglas W. "Do Dogs Resemble Their Owners? A Reanalysis of Roy and Christenfeld (2004)." *Psychological Science* 16.1 (2005).

Lévy, Arthur, and Stephen Louis Simeon. *The Private Life of Napoleon*. Vol. 1. New York: C. Scribner's Sons, 1894.

Lobell, Jarrett A., and Eric Powell. "Sacrificial Dogs." *Archaeology Magazine* (September–October 2010).

Maldarelli, Claire. "Although Purebred Dogs Can Be Best in Show, Are They Worst in Health?" *Scientific American* (February 21, 2014).

"Mexican Hairless: Breed of Dog." *Britannica*. britannica.com/animal/Mexican-hairless-dog.

Mott, Maryann. "Guard Dogs: Newfoundlands' Lifesaving Past, Present." *National Geographic* (February 7, 2003).

Mowry, William A., and Arthur May Mowry. *American Inventions and Inventors*. New York: Silver, Burdett, and Co., 1910.

"Naked Came the Werewolf." British Library *Medieval Manuscripts Blog,* February 13, 2013. britishlibrary.typepad.co.uk/digitisedmanuscripts/2013/02/naked-came-the-werewolf.html.

"Nipper and His Master's Voice." *Library and Archives Canada*. collectionscanada.gc.ca/gramophone/028011-3006.2-e.html.

Page, Jake. *Dogs: A Natural History*. New York: Smithsonian/Harper Collins, 2007.

Paré, Ambroise, and Thomas Johnson. *The Works of That Famous Chirurgion Ambrose Parey, Translated out of Latine and Compared with the French. By Th. Johnson*. London: Printed by Th. Cotes and R. Young, 1634.

"Pete the Bulldog Gets a Victim." *New York Times,* May 10, 1907.

Picard, Liza. *Elizabeth's London: Everyday Life in Elizabethan London*. New York: St. Martin's, 2003.

Pickeral, Tamsin. *The Dog: 5000 Years of the Dog in Art*. London: Merrell, 2008.

"Plebian Pup Beats White House Pete; Bull Terrier, With No Sign of Mollycoddle, Thrashes President's Pride ..." *New York Times,* May 11, 1907. query.nytimes.com/gst/abstract.html?res=9E01E3DD133EE033A25752C1A9639C946697D6C.

Pope, A. *Letters of Mr. Pope, and Several Eminent Persons, from the Year 1705, to 1711, Volume 1,* printed and sold by the booksellers of London and Westminster, 1735.

Select Bibliography CONTINUED

Ratliff, Evan. "Taming the Wild." *National Geographic* (March 2011). ngm.nationalgeographic.com/2011/03/taming-wild-animals/ratliff-text.

"Remembering Canine Cosmonauts Belka and Strelka." *Discovery* (August 19, 2015). news.discovery.com/animals/remembering-canine-cosmonauts-belka-and-strelka-150819.htm.

"Robert Peary: To the Top of the World." American Experience series. PBS. pbs.org/wgbh/amex/ice/sfeature/peary.html.

Rothmans, Lily. "This Is What Happened to the First Person to Get the Rabies Vaccine." *Time* (July 6, 2015).

Roy, Michael M., and Nicholas J. S. Christenfeld. "Do Dogs Resemble Their Owners?" *Psychological Science* 15.5 (2004), 83–84. psy2.ucsd.edu/~nchristenfeld/Publications_files/Dogs.pdf.

Schor, Jacob. "The Smell of Cancer." *Denvernaturopathic.com* (May 22, 2014). www.denvernaturopathic.com/smell-of-cancer.htm.

Schwartz, Marion. "A History of Dogs in the Early Americas." *New York Times*, July 30, 2015.

"Seaman." PBS. pbs.org/lewisandclark/inside/seaman.html.

Shea, Rachel Hartigan. "What Wide Origins You Have, Little Red Riding Hood!" *National Geographic* (November 30, 2013).

Smith, Leef. "A Bite and Bark That Saved a Life." *Washington Post*, June 19, 2006.

Smith, Lisa. "The Problem of Mad Dogs in the Eighteenth Century." *The Sloane Letters Blog*, January 27, 2014. sloaneletters.com.

Snell, Paul. British Library *Medieval Manuscripts Blog*, November 13, 2013. britishlibrary.typepad.co.uk/digitisedmanuscripts/2013/02/naked-came-the-werewolf.html.

Spackman, Thomas. *A Declaration of Such Greiuous Accidents as Commonly Follow the Biting of Mad Dogges, Together with the Cure Thereof, by Thomas Spackman Doctor of Physick.* London: Printed for Iohn Bill, 1613.

Speck, F. G. "Dogs of the Labrador Indians." *Natural History* 25.1 (1925), 58.

Speck, Frank G. *Penobscot Man: The Life History of a Forest Tribe in Maine.* Orono: University of Maine, 1997.

"Sputnik 2." NASA's National Space Science Data Center. nssdc.gsfc.nasa.gov/nmc/spacecraftDisplay.do?id=1957-002A.

Stall, Sam. *100 Dogs Who Changed Civilization: History's Most Influential Canines.* Philadelphia, Pa.: Quirk, 2007.

Swabe, Joanna. *Animals, Disease and Human Society: Human-Animal Relations and the Rise of Veterinary Medicine.* London: Routledge, 1999.

Taylor, George B. *Man's Friend, the Dog; a Treatise upon the Dog, with Information as to the Value of the Different Breeds, and the Best Way to Care for Them.* New York: Frederick A. Stokes, 1891.

Thurston, Mary Elizabeth. *The Lost History of the Canine Race: Our 15,000-year Love Affair With Dogs.* Kansas City, Mo.: Andrews and McMeel, 1996.

Toussenel, A. *L'Esprit des bêtes* Paris: Librairie phalanstérienne, 1853.

Trut, Lyudmila. "Early Canid Domestication: The Farm-Fox Experiment." *American Scientist* 87.2 (1999), 160.

"U.S. Pet Ownership Statistics." American Veterinary Medical Association. avma.org/KB/Resources/Statistics/Pages/Market-research-statistics-US-pet-ownership.aspx.

Viegas, Jennifer. "The Most Popular Dog Names in the U.S. Are ..." August 26, 2015. seeker.com/the-most-popular-dog-names-in-the-us-are-1770168293.html.

The Voyage of Martin Pring, 1603. American Journeys collection, document AJ-040. Wisconsin Historical Society Digital Archives. americanjourneys.org/aj-040/summary/index.asp.

Walker-Meikle, Kathleen. *Medieval Dogs.* London: British Library, 2013.

Wells, William Van De. *Life and Public Services of Samuel Adams.* Vol. 2. Boston: Little Brown, 1865.

Wendt, Lloyd M. *Dogs: A Historical Journey: The Human/Dog Connection Through the Centuries.* New York: Howell Book House, 1996.

"The Whole Story." Institut Pasteur. pasteur.fr/en/institut-pasteur/history/louis-pasteur/louis-pasteur-s-work/whole-story.

Withey, Alun. "Mad Dog (Bites) and Englishmen: Early-Modern Remedies for Hydrophobia." February 7, 2014. dralun.wordpress.com/2014/02/07/mad-dog-bites-and-englishmen-early-modern-remedies-for-hydrophobia.

Wynkfield, Robert. *The Execution of Mary Queen of Scots 8 February 1587.* tudorhistory.org/primary/exmary.html.

Yong, Ed. "A New Origin Story for Dogs: The First Domesticated Animals May Have Been Tamed Twice." *The Atlantic,* June 2, 2016.

Rufferences

The source of each quotation is listed here. The citation indicates the first words of the quotation.

Page 26: "fear for your stalls a midnight thief ..." (Virgil, *Georgics* LCL 63: 204-205, via loebclassics.com.

Page 26: "among the first things ..." Varro: De Re Rustica VII.11.1 Loeb Classical Library, 1934.

Page 41: "Turnspetes ... taught to dance to the drums and to the lyre." Caius, J., as cited in Barber-Lomax, J. W., *De Canibus Britannicis*, *Journal of Small Animal Practice,* Volume 1, Issue 1-4, 24–31, February 1960.

Page 42: "There is also this day among us ..." Caius, J. *Englishe Dogges*, trans. Fleming, 15, via archive.org/details/ofenglishedogges00caiuuoft.

Page 43: "espied her little dog ..." as recorded by Robert Wynkfield, 1587 via tudor history.org.

Page 49: "render'd it very offensive ..." Diary of John Evelyn, vol. 2, ed. William Bray, via archive.org/details/diaryof johnevely02eveliala.

Page 50: "We brought from Bristoll .... great and fearfull Mastives ... turned all to a jest and sport" from *The Voyage of Martin Pring*, 1603, Wisconsin Historical Society Digital Archives, via americanjourneys .org/pdf/AJ-040.pdf.

Page 52: "The more one gets to know ..." Toussenel, A. *L'Esprit des bêtes* (1847) ch. 3.

Page 52: "histories are more full ... " Letters of Mr. Pope, and Several Eminent Persons, from the Year 1705, to 1711, Volume 1, printed and sold by the booksellers of London and Westminster, 1735.

Page 52: "Mark but this flea ... " John Donne, "The Flea," 1633, poetryfoundation.org/poems-and-poets/poems/detail/46467.

Page 55: "because they feed upon carrion ..." Ambroise Paré, *The Workes of That Famous Chirurgeon* ... London, 1634, 785-86, via archive.org.

Page 55: "hath sparkling and fierie eies ..." Paré, 785-86.

Page 55: "for as long as ye party can bear it." As quoted in Withey, Alun, *Mad Dog (bites) and Englishmen: Early-modern Remedies for Hydrophobia*, February 7, 2014, dralun.word press.com/2014/02/07/ mad-dog-bites-and-englishmen-early-modern-remedies-for-hydrophobia.

Page 57: "General Washington's compliments ..." Letter from George Washington to General William Howe, 6 October 1777, founders.archives.gov/ documents/Washington/ 03-11-02-0432.

Page 57: "servants to Ladies of ..." Anon., *Low Life London 1765* as quoted in *Liza Picard, Dr. Johnson's London*, 219.

Page 59: "And our little girl, Tricia ..." Torricelli, Robert et al. *In Our Own Words: Extraordinary Speeches of the American Century*, New York, Simon and Schuster, 2000, 195.

Page 63: "dogge of the new-foundland breed" September 11, 1803, Lewisandclarkjournals .unl.edu.

Page 64: *"Millions of kisses ... Bring him ..."* Levy, Arthur, *The Private Life of Napoleon*, Vol. I, New York, Scribner and Sons, 1894, 190.

Page 69: "No one would plant weeds ..." Taylor, George B. *Man's Friend the Dog*, New York, Frederick A. Stokes Company, 1891, 7.

Page 102: "Bow-Wow" from Coren, Stanley, *How Dogs Bark in Different Languages*, November 16, 2012, psychology today.com.

To Dig Up More Sources

Books for Young Readers

Bausum, Ann. *Stubby the War Dog: The True Story of World War I's Bravest Dog.* Washington, D.C.: National Geographic Kids, 2014.

Castaldo, Nancy F. *Sniffer Dogs: How Dogs (and Their Noses) Save the World.* New York: Houghton Mifflin Harcourt, 2014.

Clutton-Brock, Juliet. *Eyewitness Dog.* New York: DK Publishing, 2014.

Gorrell, Gena K. *Working Like a Dog: The Story of Working Dogs Through History.* Toronto, Ontario: Tundra, 2003.

Patent, Dorothy Hinshaw. *Dogs on Duty: Soldiers' Best Friends on the Battlefield and Beyond.* New York: Bloomsbury, 2012.

Patent, Dorothy Hinshaw. *Super Sniffers: Dog Detectives on the Job.* New York: Bloomsbury, 2014.

Pringle, Laurence. *Dog of Discovery.* Honesdale, Pa.: Boyds Mills Press, 2002.

Books of General Interest

Derr, Mark. *Dog's Best Friend: Annals of the Dog-Human Relationship.* New York: Henry Holt, 1997.

Derr, Mark. *A Dog's History of America: How Our Best Friend Explored, Conquered, and Settled a Continent.* New York: North Point, 2004.

Grier, Katherine C. *Pets in America: A History.* Chapel Hill: University of North Carolina, 2006.

Lemish, Michael G. *War Dogs: A History of Loyalty and Heroism.* Washington, D.C.: Brassey's, 1999.

Orlean, Susan. *Rin Tin Tin: The Life and Legend.* New York: Simon and Schuster, 2011.

Thurston, Mary Elizabeth. *The Lost History of the Canine Race: Our 15,000-year Love Affair With Dogs.* Kansas City, Mo.: Andrews and McMeel, 1996.

Walker-Meikle, Kathleen. *Medieval Dogs.* London: British Library, 2013.

Wendt, Lloyd M. *Dogs: A Historical Journey: The Human/Dog Connection Through the Centuries.* New York: Howell Book House, 1996.

To Sniff Out Places to Visit

Grab a parent or guardian to check out these other great places to visit.

American Kennel Club Kids' Corner
This great resource for kids includes games, resources, a newsletter, and even an advice column. *akc.org/kids-corner*

ASPCA
Find information about adopting and caring for a dog here. *aspca.org*

Assistance Dogs
This organization trains assistance dogs for people with disabilities. The mission is to increase awareness of the rights and roles of assistance dog teams through education and advocacy. *pawswithacause.org*

The Dog & Horse Fine Art & Portraiture Gallery
If you love artwork that features animals, this gallery, located in Charleston, South Carolina, U.S.A., features hundreds of horse- and dog-themed works of art by celebrated American and European artists with varying styles. *dogandhorsefineart.com*

The Dog Collar Museum: Leeds Castle, Kent, England
If you can travel to Kent, England, visit this beautiful castle built in the 12th century. It has a collection of more than 100 collars through the ages. *leeds-castle.com/Attractions*

Lewis and Clark and the Dog, Seaman
You can find more information about Seaman and the Expedition here. *LewisandClark.org*

Museum of the Dog
Located in St. Louis, Missouri, the American Kennel Club museum has a large collection of artwork devoted to the dog through the ages. *museumofthedog.org*

The National World War I Museum and Memorial
Located in Kansas City, Missouri, U.S.A., the museum includes an exhibit about Stubby. *theworldwar.org*

Presidential Pet Museum
Located in Annapolis, Maryland, U.S.A., the museum's exhibits highlight past and current White House pets, and include little-known facts about the animals that lived at the White House. *presidentialpetmuseum.com*

Wolf Conservation Center
The Wolf Conservation Center (WCC) is a private, not-for-profit environmental education organization located in South Salem, New York. You can learn about wolves, their relationship to the environment, and the human role in protecting their future, in person or online. *nywolf.org*

Index

Index

Illustration Credits

Dedication

To Abby, Freddie, Igor, Otis, Cedar, Biscoe, Rufus, Alice,
Lyle, Flynn, Bruno, Scout, Gus, Misty, and especially Rosie.

Since 1888, the National Geographic Society has
funded more than 12,000 research, exploration,
and preservation projects around the world.
The Society receives funds from National
Geographic Partners, LLC, funded in part by your
purchase. A portion of the proceeds from this
book supports this vital work. To learn more,
visit natgeo.com/info.

For more information, visit nationalgeographic.
com, call 1-800-647-5463, or write to the following
address:

National Geographic Partners
1145 17th Street N.W.
Washington, D.C. 20036-4688 U.S.A.

Visit us online at nationalgeographic.com/books

For librarians and teachers: ngchildrensbooks.org

More for kids from National Geographic:
kids.nationalgeographic.com

For information about special discounts for bulk
purchases, please contact National Geographic
Books Special Sales: specialsales@natgeo.com

For rights or permissions inquiries, please
contact National Geographic Books Subsidiary
Rights: bookrights@natgeo.com

Designed by Marty Ittner

Library of Congress Cataloging-in-Publication Data

Names: Albee, Sarah, author. | National
    Geographic Society (U.S.)
Title: Dog days of history / by Sarah Albee.
Description: Washington, D.C. : National
    Geographic Kids, [2018] | Audience:
    Ages 9-12. | Audience: Grades 4 to 6. |
    Includes index.
Identifiers: LCCN 2017010529| ISBN
    9781426329715 (hardcover : alk. paper) |
    ISBN 9781426329722 (hardcover : alk. paper)
Subjects: LCSH: Dogs--History--Juvenile litera-
    ture. | Dogs--Anecdotes--Juvenile literature.
Classification: LCC SF426.5 .A428 2018 |
    DDC 636.7--dc23
LC record available at https://lccn.loc.gov/
    2017010529

*The publisher wishes to thank everyone who
helped make this book possible: Ariane Szu-Tu,
associate editor; Sarah J. Mock, senior photo
editor; Becky Baines, executive editor; and Scott
Vehstedt, fact-checker.*

Printed in Hong Kong
17/THK/1